Helen Gillespie-Peck

Winewoman's
Guide to Bergerac

Published by

MELROSE BOOKS

An Imprint of Melrose Press Limited
St Thomas Place, Ely
Cambridgeshire
CB7 4GG, UK
www.melrosebooks.com

FIRST EDITION

Cover designed by Sophie Fitzjohn

ISBN 978 1 905226 78 8

Printed and bound in Great Britain by:
Biddles, King's Lynn. Norfolk PE30 4LS

Contents

Chapter 1

History of Bergerac

In 1975, as was usual then, French neighbours invited us out to Sunday lunch. Living in a village just south of Bergerac, we drove towards town and just before descending the long hill, which is the main road between Bergerac and Eymet, we turned into the car park of La Grappe d'Or [Bunch of Golden Grapes], on the opposite side of the road to the restaurant. The restaurant is roughly just eight minutes from Bergerac on the road to Mont de Marsan.

The view over the Dordogne Valley was, and still is, magnificent. My French friend told me that the Dordogne River at this point was once very wide and was named the Lagoon of the Bay of Biscay. The river has somewhat receded but left a large area of mineral deposits in the soil on the land which is now called the Plains of Bergerac and is the district of St Laurent des Vignes.

In my first book, I mentioned Bergerac but gave very little information about it as I had so much more to write about many of the vineyards in France, Spain, Portugal and Italy which I had visited during my time of taking groups on coach tours to study wine. Studying wine is like playing golf – it becomes a bug you can't get rid of and you want to do more and more.

For those of you who have read the first book, you may find a little necessary repetition in this second book and I apologise for this.

Now I have the wine tours well recorded, I want to concentrate on Bergerac, after all, this is my home and has been for the last thirty years. I am truly attached to it and the people who live here.

The Dordogne is one of the largest and principal gastronomic regions of France. Philip Oyler, author of *The Green Earth* described it as: 'the richest and poorest region of France'.

Bergerac is an agricultural region which can boast not only wine production but also an excellent growing area for fruit, vegetables, nuts and even tobacco! The majority of people in the area are employed in the wine industry and agriculture, and although the average wage is very low the Bergeracois live and eat exceptionally well!

The climate is similar to Britain but warmer. There is certainly more sun, and 'summer days' start earlier and finish later in the year – sometimes into early November, making winter shorter and more bearable. The average rainfall is a little less than in the UK and this is what makes the Dordogne Valley so lusciously green. When I have brought wine enthusiasts to study the region, the same comment has arisen many times: "It's so much like parts of Devon".

Bergerac was almost unknown in the seventies; I remember reading in a guide book the description of the town: 'Sleepy little market town – not worth stopping'. That was certainly written by someone who hadn't visited the place because even at that time there were lots of interesting things happening. A land of wealth – perhaps not financially – but certainly in what the land had to offer because of the agreeable climate and the agriculturists living here.

It was at the time when holidaying in Spain was very cheap and people would drive hundreds of miles from the ferry ports in the north, through France and into Spain. Many of them came through Bergerac. There were no autoroutes and you had the

laborious job of getting through the towns, which could take an age – especially on Saturday market day – the busiest day of the week for holidaymakers.

I always remember having to tackle the traffic in Tours – it could take nearly an hour to get through to the other side. You drove into the centre and then had to get across the bridge; it took ages and then you had to join the traffic crawling along the road running beside the Loire before getting to the south side of the town. The traffic on the main roads between the towns was almost as bad; lorries galore could hold you up for long periods.

What with these driving conditions and it becoming hotter as you drove south, tempers began to fray. It was a welcome relief when you had dealt with the traffic in Angoulême and proceeded into the Dordogne region. Of course, you don't realise how big the region is and it took two to three hours to get to Bergerac.

In those days, the travel time was around fourteen hours from the ports, either Le Havre or Caen, to my home. Nowadays, when I drive from Bergerac to Roscoff – which is further – I can do it in seven and a half hours! Once you get onto the autoroute, north of Libourne – it's autoroute right into the port!

Anyway, let's get back to the holidaymakers driving through Bergerac to get to Spain. It was strange what happened later and I observed it with great interest.

The cost of accommodation, food and drink in Spain gradually mounted – which the British soon noticed – and the difference in the cost of holidaying in France compared with Spain decreased. Perhaps the long drive was also taking its toll – even with two drivers, non-stop is no fun!

All of a sudden, people started to stay overnight in the few hotels available in Bergerac – or even camped, as we have some lovely camp sites along the Dordogne. If you had a caravan it was even easier because there is no charge for stopping overnight in suitable parking areas at the side of the road, and in Bergerac we have an ideal parking area alongside the Dordogne. That was the start of Bergerac becoming a tourist centre.

With the increase in population and the number of tourists visiting this market town, our little bridge was having problems coping with it all and a decision was taken to build another more or less alongside [about 300 metres between them both] to relieve what was then becoming congestion in the town, which was once smaller than Monbazillac! The new bridge was a great success because not only did it alleviate the traffic but from it the view of the old bridge, at the right time of day, with the sun shining on it and the reflection on the river is absolutely stunning!

Yes, Bergerac was coming together.

Aquitaine is the region of the south-west of France, the name means 'land of waters' and that's just what it is. Dordogne is a department within Aquitaine and here one can see this excellent evidence of river layout. The Dordogne River gets its name from its source in the Massif Central in the Auvergne region on Mont Dore – the golden mountain.

Digressing just a little bit – if you get the chance to taste the cheese of Mont Dore do so, it's wonderful! It is a seasonal cheese [autumn months] and I would describe it as a 'Camembert soufflé' with lots more flavour. Now back to the rivers…

The Dordogne flows through Bergerac to Libourne. Here it joins up with the river L'Isle and they meander happily together to just north of Bordeaux – in line with Château Margaux. At this point it joins the Garonne, which flows through the Lot-et-Garonne and eventually into Bordeaux. The brown, muddy Garonne is the river on which Bordeaux stands.

Now we have to return to Libourne where we find the confluence of the Dordogne and the river L'Isle. This is a very important point of the river structure of Aquitaine when looking at the historic economics of the wine trade of this region.

Barrels of wine were shipped from Bergerac to Libourne, then loaded onto larger boats which took the wine to Bordeaux and beyond. Henry Plantagenet depended on the loyalty of the winemakers of Bergerac to supply the wine for onward shipment. I suppose many of you know about this, but what you may not know is that the river L'Isle was also of great importance.

The L'Isle, not mentioned much when discussing the Dordogne, runs from the north through the Limousin region where the best oak in France can be found. It is much in demand especially in Bordeaux. The boats carried the oak from the Limousin southwards to Bordeaux to make barrels. These were made in many parts of the region so some of the wood was unloaded in Libourne as well as Bordeaux. The boats were then loaded with large cargoes of wine for the return voyage to Perigueux and beyond.

It is a great pity that the Dordogne is no longer navigable and a defence barrier has been built just outside Bergerac which you can visit by pleasure boat in the summer months. Just think of the tourist industry we could have had on the three rivers if the Dordogne had remained passable.

Libourne, the administration centre and port for wines of the south-west, was strategically placed so that exchanges of cargo could be made with the boats from Bergerac. It is reckoned perhaps a quarter of wine exports from Libourne and Bordeaux came to England during this time.

The port, founded in 1269, was named after Roger Leyburn, an Englishman, a baron from Kent and a close friend of King

Edward I. He was appointed steward of the Royal Household. At one stage he was at odds with Edward who believed Leyburn was guilty of embezzlement, but at the battle of Kenilworth in 1265 he saved Edward's life, thus redeeming himself. He was King Edward's lieutenant when Edward was made warden of the Cinque Ports. From 1266 Leyburn was Edward's lieutenant in Gascony with full powers. He died in 1271.

Leyburn was also responsible for building the property of Cheval-Blanc, the premier *Grand Cru classé* property of St Emilion. It was built originally as a coach house for the wine buyers who came to the region. You can just imagine it – The White Horse Inn!

Well, Bergerac may have been a place 'not worth stopping off' in *but* the original Mr Berry [of Berry Bros] didn't think that way. I read that he had visited Bergerac in the thirties and stayed in one of the hotels, where he encountered one or two rats in his bedroom during the night – not a pleasant experience!

I can understand this because when I first came to Bergerac, the old part of the town was not a place to visit in the heat of the summer. There was a continual, overwhelming stench in the narrow streets with pools of stagnant water, dogs' excrement and loads of litter. You could have bought an apartment there for next to nothing! The whole area had been absolutely neglected and I often wondered why Bergerac had not been restored like the centre of Sarlat, a medieval town further east along the Dordogne. Because of this restoration, Sarlat was flooded with tourists in the summer.

Later, when there was evidence of more tourists coming to Bergerac and certainly more British people moving into the area, things started to happen. The Church of St James [Jacques] in the centre of the old town was restored and the front of the church was cleared to make way for a paved square which is now surrounded by restaurants and art shops. It is a wonderful setting in the summer, with the restaurants spilling over into the square with pretty tables set for either lunch or dinner. August is a month which shouldn't be missed and musical entertainment is also provided. The church stands proudly overlooking this square.

It has taken a few years to restore, but progress has been made and most of the old buildings have been renovated offering a centre or should I say *vieux quartier* with many interesting shops where you can spend much more time than you ever thought. It is worthwhile noting that property for sale around the *vieux quartier* is now more difficult to acquire and an apartment is quite expensive these days.

In the seventies there was only one bridge over the Dordogne at Bergerac, but this wasn't the first. The original bridge was built in the Middle Ages and the remains can still be seen today. If you stand on the west side of the old bridge, facing south, you can see where the original bridge stood. In fact, near where you are standing you will see a street called Rue de l' Ancien Pont and this is the road which led from the bridge into the little town of Bergerac.

Even the old monastery, which now houses the CIVRB (Conseil Interprofessional des Vins de la Région de Bergerac) had a facelift. The old tasting lab where I spent time learning something about viticulture was closed and another rebuilt, and we can boast a fine wine-tasting auditorium. Then a massive rebuilding project came into force – an upper floor facing the river to house the laboratory and offices. The old building below was completely restored and offers an exhibition room, conference rooms, etc. The cost of this work must have been enormous.

It was from here that the monks ventured to Rome, extolling the wonders of the wine of Monbazillac, and when asked by the Pope where they had come from they said a little town called Bergerac, near Monbazillac!

The grounds inside the former monastery are used in the summer for concerts and lunches – such as that of the Concours d'Elegance d'Automobiles Classiques held in June.

Michel Delpon has written an interesting book on the wines of Bergerac, entitled *Les Vins de Bergerac*. Unfortunately, it is in French and unless the tourist's French is good enough he or she might have difficultly understanding it.

In 768 Charlemagne ruled here and called Bergerac 'The peaceful province'. Later, a Comte du Perigord was created.

In 1080 a Benedictine priest was installed at the Château of Bergerac, which was built on the right side of the river to control the river traffic. The population in this fertile valley also increased. In 1209 the first bridge was built over the Dordogne at Bergerac and is referred to in another part of this book.

Henry III was also very fond of the wines of Bergerac. In 1254 he relied on the loyalty of the Bergeracois to ensure their wines travelled safely from Bergerac to Libourne.

In 1322 Bergerac vineyards were 'marked out' by the Coutumes de Bergerac. Once a vineyard area is defined it will be demarcated. On the right bank these stretched for 10–15 kilometres including Ginestat, Maurens, Camsegret, Lembras, Creysse and Mouleydier.

A tax was introduced by the Count of Perigueux which was not accepted by the majority of winegrowers on the north bank of the Dordogne and many moved to the south bank. On the 4th September 1495 the vineyards of the south of Bergerac passed before the Parliament of Bordeaux for demarcation.

It is interesting to note that in the 17th century the date of the *vendange* came later in the year – and this was simply to satisfy the 'Noble Rot'.

There was a time when Bergerac had thirty taverns and the wine flowed, although the sale was regulated for the peasants – only consuls and mayors were exempt. You knew if a tavern sold wine as there was a Seneschal on the door of the tavern bearing official names.

In 1326 under the reign of King Charles, the Seigneur of Bergerac, Renaud de Pons, instituted a marque for wines to be exported. It is described as 'pied de griffon' [foot of a fountain or spring]. Also each barrel had a pail fitted to the side – what for, I have no idea.

Montcuq is one of the most important villages in the history of Bergerac. It is not far from Château Monplaisir and when I discuss it with the locals who have lived here all their lives it seems that no one has even visited it. Of course, there is very little left as the church was taken down and all the stones have disappeared.

This little site is where the Hundred Years' War started with the arrival in this area of the English army led by the Count of Derby, Selon Froissart. The English actually spent the night here and drank some of the good wines of Bergerac.

During this war, Bergerac was successfully defended by the English, the Gascons and the *arbalétriers* [archers] on the 26th August 1345. Led by Henry of Grosmont and Sir Walter Manny, the French were defeated at Bergerac, as well as at La Reole, Montsegur, Aiguillon and Angoulême – though the latter was quickly regained by the French. Edward III granted Henry of Grosmont, later of Lancaster, the castle and town of Bergerac which he had captured. From the profits earned there Henry built the Palace of the Savoy in London. This would be destroyed and its furnishings burned by the actions of a mob and gunpowder in the 1380s.

South of Bergerac is a village high on a hill where if you are there when the *militaire* from Bordeaux practise low flying exercises, you can actually see the pilot's face! It is here in the ruin of the chateau you will find a cannonball or two used in the

Hundred Years' War.

The soil was rich in Lamonzie St Martin and St Laurent des Vins. In the 12th century they started cultivating the vine in this region. Legend has it that the Noble Rot was discovered here – before Sauternes. I have heard so many stories about the origin of Noble Rot that I am now completely confused. This one tells us of how St Martin was too occupied with other things and allowed the fungus, Noble Rot, to set in. Refusing to lose any of the benefits of producing wine, he went ahead with the harvest on Mont Bazillac and, according to this legend, that was the birth of the wine we now know as Monbazillac.

In 1209 Bergerac became an important point in the Valley of the Dordogne. It was also en route for the pilgrims travelling to St Jacques de Compostella. Bergerac was now an important port and, during the Plantagenets' time, the wines of Bergerac were in demand for shipping up to the north.

Château Monbazillac is surely the most popular attraction in Bergerac and this is why I now apologise to anyone who has read my first book. It is necessary for me to repeat my story of this chateau as this book is a guide to Bergerac.

Since 1980 I have been a regular visitor – either by accompanying small groups or just taking my friends. It has changed a lot in recent years.

The first Château Monbazillac was built by Catholics and it wasn't long after that when it was burned down and then rebuilt by the Protestants. It then became a Protestant stronghold and was very much involved in the War of Religions. Since then, peace has prevailed and this beautiful chateau stands proudly on the hills overlooking the Dordogne Valley.

Until around 1960, the chateau was owned privately, then it was sold to the Co-operative of Monbazillac who furnished it with help from people in the houses nearby – many had collections of bibles, coins and maps which they handed over for the 'museum'.

Visits at that time were interesting, there seemed to be more to see and this gave you a very good idea how Bergerac and its environs had originated. For example, there was a room full of old maps and from these you could see how small Bergerac was in comparison to Monbazillac and La Calevie nearby. It was no wonder that when the monks of the monastery of Bergerac went to see the Pope in Rome and were asked where they had come from, their reply was, "a small village outside Monbazillac"! This room had a door into one of the towers and this small area was used as a prison in times of war. It has a small window and a stone seat where the prisoner was left to die. Such cruel times!

The two reception rooms give you an excellent example of the furniture made and the wood available in the region. The floor of one is laid with four different woods and the beams have flowers and other designs painted on them.

The Religious room has an amazing collection of Calvin Bibles and literature of the period, as well as a fair collection of coins which have been found on the land around. Some of these coins are extremely valuable and, because of this, the originals were taken to Paris and only copies remain in the chateau.

From this room, you go through a small door leading into part of the tower. In this room there is a family tree painted on the walls. The name Rudel appears in the early part of the chateau's existence, and he may well have been one of the first troubadours during the period of Eleanor of Aquitaine.

I was once told – and whether it is true or not I'm not sure – but a troubadour called Rudel wrote a song about his love who was 'far away'. Eleanor took it to be a song about her and he was favoured to travel with her to the Holy Lands. Later, it was discovered that he did have a far-away lover – but it wasn't Eleanor!

Before going upstairs, there is a room where you will find machinery used in trades of the past and this includes rope manufacturing, clog making and barrel production.

One room upstairs is laid out as a dining room, furnished with very heavy furniture of the Baroque period which had been given 'on loan' to the château by Monet Sully, the Perigordin 'Shakespeare actor'. The family never asked for it to be returned – probably because it was so difficult to clean.

The room of photographs showing Dordogne chateaux was

just as interesting because it demonstrated to visitors that there are probably more chateaux on the Dordogne than on the Loire, the difference being that Dordogne chateaux were built for war, and those on the Loire were built for pleasure by the followers of the Kings of France. Many of the villages in the surrounding Dordogne were called *bastides* and these were held by either the Protestants or the Catholics – some actually changed from one church to the other.

The Lady's bedroom is furnished in local furniture of different styles, in particular is the incomplete prayer desk of Italian style. The bed is very small, but seemingly they preferred to sleep in a sitting-up position.

The last room on this floor is devoted to the Perigordin painter Sem, who lived at the same time as his friend Toulouse Lautrec. It is obvious from Sem's work that he was a great admirer of Lautrec's paintings as his work characterises the very well-known thin men and fat ladies of Paris. It never ceases to amaze me why the chateau has never made copies of his work for the public to buy – especially the one produced for Maxim's in Paris which Sem frequented.

Down in the cellar is the kitchen; this to me was one of the most interesting rooms to visit. Apart from the many pots for storing walnut oil, pork fat, etc., which had been donated by those living around the chateau, everything else was original. There is a door leading from the kitchen into the lower part of one of the towers, this was the fridge. The water would drip in and settle on the floor and freeze so food could be stored in here. In the kitchen itself, there was a well so they were never without water. Bread was baked in this kitchen; the oven with its concave ceiling of red bricks is worth looking into; once the fire was lit, it became very hot. Outside the oven there are two holes, one on each side, which have been filled in with large stones. These holes were for storing salt and keeping it dry. Salt was a valuable commodity – especially during the time of Louis XIV. In order for him to get more money to pay for his armies he put a tax on salt!

Adjacent to the kitchen is a cellar where the famous Monbazillac sweet wine was produced, then stored for many years.

As we were guided through the chateau, we were shown a photograph of the Queen Mother when she visited the chateau. The guide told us that she had come to Bergerac to order some Monbazillac. This joke possibly arose from the time when the sweet wine of Sauternes went to the Tsars of Russia and the Monbazillac wines to the Royal Household in London.

The lady who looks after the chateau is Italian. She no longer takes groups on tour through the chateau. The last time I saw her she was sitting at the reception desk in the entrance hall.

There has always been a degree of mystery regarding Cyrano de Bergerac. Some people truly believed Cyrano de Bergerac was actually a man from these parts. Even now they are upset when told that he, as Cyrano, a man of Bergerac, didn't exist as such. He was, in a way, a figment of the imagination created by Edmund Rostand around a poet called Cyrano who lived south

of Paris. Rostand was born in 1868 in Marseille, but went to Paris to study law. However, his interest in literature soon took over. In 1897 he wrote *Cyrano de Bergerac* for the greatest French comic actor of the time, Coquelin the elder. It was a winner! Rostand was made a Chevalier de la Legion d'Honneur within days of the play's premiere. From then on it was 'downhill' and due to ill health he retired to the Pyrenees. He died in Paris in 1918. It is available as an Oxford World's Classic, translated by Christopher Fry into English for the Oxford University Press.

When Cyrano reached a suitable age, he was called into the *militaire* – much against his wishes. As he was an educated man, he was given what we nowadays call 'direct entry' and went straight into the *militaire* as an officer.

Such a wonderful, sympathetic love story about Cyrano, who had the misfortune to have a big nose. He fell in love with a young, beautiful girl called Roxanne, but she couldn't return his love as she had already fallen in love with one of the young soldiers, called Christian. This soldier was actually one of Cyrano's men – unknown to him at that time.

Cyrano was heartbroken, but later the pain was eased because Christian, not as literate as Cyrano, was wounded and unable to answer the love letters sent to him by Roxanne. He went to Cyrano for help.

Cyrano agreed to write the letters for him, and in time Cyrano was able to express his love for Roxanne through these letters. This helped to heal Cyrano's broken heart – or so the story goes…

Roxanne fell madly in love – not so much with the soldier but with the writer of the love letters – thinking it was the young soldier. Later she was to find out that it was actually Cyrano who had written the letters.

Cyrano: "What's wrong with you?"
Christian: "She doesn't love me anymore".
Cyrano: "No?"
Christian: "It's you, it's you she loves!"

Cyrano de Bergerac has been the symbol of Bergerac wines for many years, and in the eighties, accompanied by his nose, you would find him on the labels of wine bottles. People continued to believe that he was a real person! I was often asked where he lived... Some of the best publicity for Bergerac wine was when his nose was equated to the wines of Bergerac. 'Our wines have a big nose' and Cyrano's *nez* was close by.

In the old part of Bergerac there is a statue of him. Lamentably, his nose was very rarely attached to his face as the statue was continually vandalized and the nose always suffered. Now we have, in addition, an excellent new statue of him in La Place Pélissière. It was realised by the sculptor Mauro Corda.

Edmund Rostand is commemorated by streets, a school, and so on, named after him. He didn't know it at the time but he gave Bergerac something very special which will be cherished by the town and its people forever.

Chapter 2

David Baxter

After a disastrous first marriage I had made up my mind never to marry again. That is how it stayed for over seventeen years as I had immersed my life in wine study and derived so much satisfaction from it. There was no room for anyone or anything else, that is, until I met David.

It is strange how things happen and I must tell you immediately: I'm a great believer in fate, as this chapter will prove.

Just before his former colleagues left, they saw an article in a wine journal to say that I would be in the Dordogne over the Christmas period. With this information, they contacted me and asked if it was possible for me to taste their wines as up to now it was only friends who had tasted, and they would like a truly unbiased opinion.

At first, I thought that I couldn't really be bothered working during my visit, I was in need of a rest, so made no effort to contact CMP [Château Monplaisir]. Then, just after Christmas, feeling guilty, I telephoned David to say I would call to taste his wines.

As I approached the chateau, climbing a hill with vines to the left and vines to the right, I thought that the wine might be of reasonable quality because of the good sloping vineyards. Not steep like those in Germany or the northern part of the Côtes du

Rhone, these were manageable slopes.

Although Gageac was only four kilometres from my home, I hadn't visited the village as there is very little of interest – apart from the 11th century Château Gageac, occupied by the English in 1371 with the French hero Duguesclin 'knocking at the door'. You turn off, drive up the hill and there on the right is Château Monplaisir. I was truly impressed when I entered the gates of CMP. It is a strange building in some ways; it looked like three properties joined together, as indeed it was. This was often the case in the Dordogne: it starts off as a shepherd's hut then a large room is built on, then another and so it goes on.

I can give you an excellent example of this. It happened on the road between Cunéges and Gageac Rouillac. A chap used to come here every year in his caravan for his holidays. He bought a piece of land and put a garage/shed on it. Every August, he was there, caravan with awning and a shed. It wasn't long before he built a building onto the shed, and another, so when they came on holiday there was no need to live in the caravan – they had a house. Only a year or so later, I saw a 'for sale' sign in front of the property and I happened to meet the man at the village 'summer dinner'. I asked why he was selling up so quickly after building the house. He told me that they came from the north of France and the journey getting here was becoming quite difficult each year as he got older. I say, it wasn't a bad investment!

Now back to Château Monplaisir, a building in three parts. There had definitely been an addition in about 1920 and the second part, which has a tower and a black slate roof, was added pre-war. The original building, built in two parts, also had a tower but with a red tiled roof.

When I arrived in the courtyard, I looked around. There was the winery, stockage block, tasting room and the workshop all to hand. I thought to myself then, what a super place to manage – even I could do it. I knocked on the door.

David answered, a bit dishevelled as he had visibly just woken from a nap after lunch and looking very much like an older version of the photograph of the Perigordin artist Sem, which you can see in Château Monbazillac. The large room with a dominating stone fireplace was full of books and clutter. On the table stood the different bottles of wine and a few glasses – all of the wrong type to taste wine. I wasn't too thrilled by the glasses, wrong shapes and not sparkling clean. I couldn't see one ISO type. Anyway, we got down to tasting.

The main grapes of CMP are as for Bordeaux, for the white wine, Sauvignon Blanc, Sémillon and Muscadelle. For the red wine, the grapes are Cabernet Sauvignon, Cabernet Franc, Merlot and Malbec. The Sauvignon Blanc vines are older and, if it is a good year, we make a single grape variety wine with it. The Cabernet Sauvignon vines are also old and this definitely gives the wines of CMP longevity. But there I was, sitting at a table, confronted by these wines. David, sitting opposite me, waited eagerly to hear what I had to say.

The labels were attractive and looked good, except for the Bergerac Sec. The green background on the label on a green bottle. Good design – wrong colour.

The Bergerac Sec that year had been made with Sémillon only, and on taking it to my nose I got a powerful whiff of citrus fruit and delicate flowers. As I stuck my nose into the glass the aroma seemed to soften, and just as well because on tasting it I found it a little bland at first, but developing hints of honey and tropical fruit were left in the mouth.

The Bergerac Sauvignon was something different. As I brought the glass to the 'sniff test' a subtle vinous bouquet was already heading up to the olfactory senses and on tasting it, in its entirety, I wasn't disappointed. This was a delightful, refreshing, zingy wine – with an acidity level I love to find in Bergerac Sec wine. [As a late note, we were still drinking this wine in 2002!]

The Bergerac Rosé was glorious to look at, pale raspberry in colour – so attractive that it made you want to open it and drink it! The *cépage* used was 50% Malbec [the sole grape used in traditional Cahors wine] and 50% Cabernet Sauvignon. There was a lovely aroma of strawberries and this fruitiness continued on to the palate which made me immediately think of Wimbledon, and I wondered again why rosé wine is not on sale there as an alternative to champagne with strawberries – sheer snobbism!

What pleased me most about this rosé was the level of acidity, it was low – but enough to give the wine a lovely freshness.

During the summer months when I visit my friends in Bordeaux, rosé is usually served as an aperitif and nearly always I found the higher level of acidity quite upsetting and made sure that I had only one glass. Bergerac Rosé is my choice, not only as an aperitif, but also to accompany many of the superb Perigourdin lunches in the summer. [The word Perigourdin seems to be spelt in several different ways and many don't know that it means the same as Dordogne. No one has come up with a word like 'Dordognan'!]

We don't make a lot of rosé at CMP, but we have doubled production twice in three years because of demand. It is definitely our best-seller as most is sold before it is bottled!

Back to the 'tasting' and the Côtes de Bergerac Rouge. There were two reds to taste, one 'normal' and the other which was going to be aged in French oak for twelve months. When I tasted it, it had been in oak for only one month. Bear in mind that these reds had been taken from the vat and barrel for me to taste.

The first one, the normal, was as I had expected: raw – but you could taste the fruit. It tasted like it hadn't finished its malolactic fermentation.

The malolactic fermentation turns the malic acid – like the acidity you find in green apples, which makes the wine taste 'raw' – into lactic acid which is much softer. This fermentation happens after the alcoholic fermentation.

The red wine, which had been aged in oak for only a month, was the next to taste. A little daunted by the rawness of the first red, I apprehensively took the glass to my nose. This was quite different, a nose of dark red fruits and the same fruitiness with obvious oak connotations seasoned my palate on tasting. A wine full of promise and I looked forward to tasting it when it had aged the twelve months – as is usual in the Bergerac region.

As it so happened, the 1997 normal turned out to be a very drinkable red and soon sold out. The one aged in oak was a 'late developer' and even in 2001 we were told that it wasn't quite ready! By 2003 it was one of the favourite wines in some of the best restaurants in Bergerac and its environs. Now as we come to the end of 2004, the wine is 'coming to the edge of the plateau' and, although it is still drinking well, we find the odd bottle which has gone. I rate it as one of the best wines ever produced at CMP.

Last, but not least, was the Saussignac Moelleux. I was dreading having to taste a heavy, sweet wine. I am not a lover of this style of wine, except on special occasions – as with foie gras. Only a few months before, I had taken a group to the Sauternes and had a tasting at one of the premier vineyards. The wine was outstanding – so was the price – but after the tasting, I felt the wine lying heavy inside me which caused a fair amount of discomfort.

Well, I tasted the Saussignac Moelleux and was pleasantly surprised. The nose was delicate, of fruit – all sorts of fruit. The wine was light and also delicate, with at first, a citrus taste on the palate, followed by honey and tropical fruits and had a reasonably long finish. This was certainly different and I imagined myself sitting out on a summer's evening with a glass of this chilled wine – not frozen – as an aperitif and pretending I was in the Caribbean. Because of climate conditions, this wine wasn't made again until 2000, and in that year it was awarded a gold medal.

On summing up the wines, I said to David that I thought the quality of the wine produced at CMP was good and would be even better once the work he had planned to do in the vineyards was carried out. Unlike his ex-colleague, David was accepting the advice of his winemaker, Erick, who had lots of experience not only in traditional winemaking but through discussion with other winemakers and learning through this communication. In the wine production world you learn a lot by listening…

I also suggested to David that the Sémillon be blended with some Sauvignon. In a good year like 1997 it was great to have Bergerac Sauvignon, but as we have learned over the years the Sémillon improves tremendously with the addition of Sauvignon which has a lovely acidity to lift the Sémillon out of the doldrums.

Some of the Sauvignon vines of Monplaisir are over forty years old and produce a very good wine with the ability to age. The reds speak for themselves; they are a good example of Bergerac quality reds.

After this meeting, I visited David whenever I was in the Dordogne, and started acting as his UK agent. Unless you are in the trade it is very difficult to get into the British wine market. I presented his wine at tastings whenever possible but selling Bergerac wine isn't easy. The trade price for this wine is... obscene! Yes, that's the word I would use. When you compare a wine of Bordeaux of a lesser quality demanding three times as much it makes you sick inside.

David Baxter

I don't agree with business partnerships – they've never worked out for me. My first experience was when I was asked to go into a kindergarten partnership. My partner's husband had a toy shop and all the equipment used in the kindergarten was

bought through his business. The kindergarten thrived, there was a continual waiting list, but alas, being a naval officer's wife, the time came for me to travel with my ex-husband.

When the termination of the partnership was discussed, I expected to have some compensation for the cost of the equipment for which my share of the business had paid – but I left with nothing.

Several years passed, then one day I received a letter from the 'partner'. She informed me that she had joined the Church and, before doing so, wanted my forgiveness for the way she had treated me in the termination of the partnership. There was no cheque – just a simple letter which I sympathetically answered.

The other occasion was during my wine business life. A keen wine enthusiast was taking early retirement and wanted to become involved in my business. I told him I didn't want a partner – after the last experience. He persevered and after many months I agreed as I wanted to expand and realised I would need help to do so. The idea was that he would take 50 per cent of the workload. This never happened, his wife objected to him spending time in the office, so that was the end.

The only partnership which I believe in is marriage.

David Baxter had a similar experience. He was a man with over thirty years in the City, a director of Newton Investment Management, living in Richmond, enjoying London life, theatres, cinemas, restaurants and superb book shops – all of which he frequented regularly. He came to the conclusion that if he didn't change direction in the near future, he would probably stay with Newtons until retirement and then find work in one of the charity/second-hand book shops in Richmond. He would have enjoyed being with books as he is an avid reader – the only time he isn't reading is when he is watching ancient westerns on TV, enjoying a 'wee dram', in the bath or asleep! On the other hand, it would have been extremely boring and he felt that this wasn't what he really wanted – he needed a challenge.

Well, in my book, there are 'Challenges' and 'Challenges' – and he certainly went from the sublime to the ridiculous! He took up the offer of one of his colleagues who said he would be interested in buying a farm, or such like, in France so together they went off in search of their future.

The idea was that they would go into business together. David would be financing the project at the beginning, and when the other fellow sold his farm in the UK he would contribute his share.

They found many suitable places in Gaillac and the Dordogne, but when David set his eyes on Château Monplaisir he knew it was the place he would like to own. David was the investor so the choice was his, but the colleague agreed with his decision.

After they moved in they started straight away on the vineyard because the grapes had to be harvested in just a couple of months. It was necessary to hire a couple of people to work in the vineyard [two per ten hectares is the recognised requirement] and Jeremy, an English chap, who had lived here and helped to run his parents' vineyard until they divorced and sold up, joined them. He was followed by a Frenchman, Erick, who had worked for one of the principal wine producers in Bergerac but because of difficult times in the wine business had been made redundant.

Later, Jeremy was offered a job as manager at Château Fayolle which had been taken over by Ringwood Breweries. He wanted Erick to go with him, but Erick preferred to stay with David as he would be the senior worker.

1997 was a glorious summer and gave great hope for the *vendange*. Not only were they able to produce red wine normal, red aged in *barriques*, rosé, and white Sémillon but also Sauvignon. The Sauvignon vines are older and in very good years CMP produces a Sauvignon single grape which is superb. They say that most Sauvignon Blancs don't age well but with older vines this is possible, and the 1997 Château Monplaisir Sauvignon proved this as it aged very well.

It was also a year when we produced our Saussignac Moelleux. These years are rare – we have had only three in nine years. Again, another special wine as the grapes [Sémillon] stay on the vine until they have been attacked by Noble Rot which causes the juice to become more concentrated. We then pick and ferment in the usual way but stop the fermentation before it is absolutely finished – allowing residual sugar to be left in the wine.

Both reds were good but the one aged in oak was definitely a 'late developer'. In 2001 one of the locals came to taste our wines and said that the 1997 wasn't ready for drinking! Since 2002 it has been a great favourite in the good restaurants of Bergerac.

So, considering the vineyard was in a poor state, it produced some good wines which gives wadding to what I believe in – that not only must you have a good vineyard but you must be able to carry out good repair work in the winery. The vineyards were in a poor state, but they are now the best situated in Gageac.

David's colleague wasn't very happy with the way of life here in the sticks. He – not unreasonably – got furious when every time something had to be collected from the local garage or agricultural depot, that it was necessary for the two workers, Erick and Jeremy's replacement, to hop into the van and go...I must admit, it makes me mad, even now – such a waste of man hours – but that's the way they do it here.

He was contented with the lady he chose to cook lunch and keep CMP tidy for them. When they asked around, one or two ladies offered to help. One couldn't drive a car, which wasn't much good when shopping was needed, and she wasn't nearly as good looking as the other one, who could drive. Needless to say, the good-looking one got the job.

The good-looking lady found him embarrassing and later, when I got to know her better, she told me of her embarrassment by his attentions.

Other things must have been irritating him as well because whilst David was in Scotland for his Christmas hols, he received a letter dated 3rd December from the colleague, who had also returned to the UK, in October, to look at marketing in the UK, to say that he didn't think their working relationship in the Dordogne was good – they were both stubborn people who were used to having their own way and he now believed that 'it was right when they say that you shouldn't go into business with your friends'.

In my opinion, this man didn't seem to do a lot of thinking

beforehand. They had worked together in London, they knew each other's ways, surely a future life as business partners had been thought out well by both? It was perhaps that his girlfriend didn't cherish the thought of living at Château Monplaisir, giving up a remunerative position in the UK, or another reason, which is a possibility, could have been that David had financed the project and, come the New Year, it was expected that the colleague would invest a small sum?

When I think about this, I feel here is a very selfish, weak man who, after only five months, walked out of a business partnership completely set up financially for him by David – without giving it a fair try. Perhaps there were problems but I'm sure these could have been resolved by sharing the workload; having their own responsibilities and, if they really got on each other's nerves, restoring the other property so that they could live apart. I may be wrong, but I think the colleague and his girlfriend decided they didn't want to invest in the business – and this was their way out.

Everyone was quite relieved when he left – especially the workforce. Although it was before my time, I was repeatedly

told all about 'the colleague' whose ideas were not really conducive to the 'restructuring' of Château Monplaisir and its wine production.

The colleague had suggested that the plum trees should be taken up and the land replanted with vines. The government at that time was offering a special scheme when you were paid, roughly, £4,000 per hectare for doing so. David, Jeremy and Erick disagreed with this decision and thank goodness they did because the 'plum income' is most rewarding, especially as CMP acquired its own ovens to dry and convert the plums into prunes. If this had been done it could have been disastrous for CMP because of the loss of that income. When I heard this, I did begin to wonder how much research had been done by the colleague beforehand.

For some years, France has suffered in the world wine market, and Bergerac even more as it has always been in the shadow of Bordeaux and this is reflected in the price of Bergerac wines. So making a viable business in the Bergerac wine industry is very difficult.

The plum income is, so far, a sure thing, and, to me, to suggest taking them up was something only a person with very little experience or foresight would do. I know this sounds very critical, but it is true.

I feel that neither David nor the colleague had realised what they had taken on. As David read recently, there is a quote which states: 'Buying a vineyard is like digging a deep hole and pouring money into it!' That, to me, says it all and confirms that there is certainly no room for rash decisions.

Chapter 3

Getting Together

As time went on, I realised that David and I had a lot in common, and as he had lost the help of his colleague he was beginning to depend on me more and more to help with the running of CMP – even though it was by telephone!

I decided that I couldn't continue working in Devon, I had to be within easier reach of Bergerac. So I had a choice: I could have moved up to London where there is plenty of work for wine educators or move back to France. I chose the latter.

David needed me to work with him and support him, and this I couldn't do living in Britain. So I moved back to France – while keeping a base in Devon.

Château Monplaisir was originally a house with a tremendous amount of land stretching for hectares and hectares. The house was extended around the 1920s and given a wonderful majestic façade overlooking the valley of the Dordogne and even further – the views from the terrace are similar to those seen from Château Monbazillac – the most famous of chateaux in Bergerac. This is probably how it became a chateau.

In France, anyone can call their property a 'chateau' whether it is a stone shed, house or fully blown *manoir*. In fact you will find lots of wineries with small houses calling the property a chateau; this is acceptable.

The original owner was a hard-working man and was probably responsible for making Monplaisir the vineyard you see today – but in his time it was much larger. As they say, it often happens that the son doesn't follow in his father's footsteps and this was certainly the case here. When the father died, the son took over. He wasn't really the type to run a vineyard.

He enjoyed a more modern life, and had a great love for up-to-date fast cars which is quite an expensive hobby. Selling wine was difficult, as most from Château Monplaisir was being sold off in bulk – no bottling came into the equation and sadly no profit was made. To maintain the property and the vineyards he had no alternative other than to sell off some of the hectares of land and properties.

Because of the lack of interest in Château Monplaisir, not only was the house neglected but so were the vineyards. The vineyards had suffered because there was insufficient money for maintenance. It apparently was going 'downhill' rapidly and against the wishes of his family he put it up for sale. His family included one son who was desperate for his father to keep it as he was interested in wine and Monplaisir should have been his inheritance. We have been told that the son is now working in the wine business in Bergerac and, to me, this is extremely sad. If you read Philip Oyler's book *The Generous Earth* you will find out how important land is to the people of the Dordogne.

The chateau was for sale for some time – simply because of the high price it commanded. Although neglect had set in, it wasn't insurmountable and the well-situated vineyards – probably the best in Gageac – surrounding the prominent chateau overlooking the valley were a bonus to any buyer interested in wine production. I think one of the problems may have been that the buyer with the money required for such a property would doubtless be looking nearer Bordeaux, as at that time, before air connection, Bergerac wines were still not as well known as they are today.

I heard there were wine producers in the area hoping the value would fall, so that they could afford to buy it, but, with a shock to all, David came along and fell in love with the 'location, location, location' and took over the ownership in May 1997. We heard from a local that an Englishman was very interested but was advised by an English lady not to buy it… There was also an American from Arizona who wanted to buy the chateau – but without the vineyards.

Since selling the property to David, the previous owner has been able to pursue his love – by changing his car regularly and living near Bergerac – without vines.

Agricultural land was cheap, but land with property is becoming more and more expensive now, so when you buy a vineyard you are actually paying for the increased price of property and that is the best way to assess the value.

When David moved in, the chateau had been virtually stripped. This is common in France – except in properties where the owner has died. He had well and truly bought bare walls – some falling down! All electric light fittings had been removed, leaving wires hanging from the ceiling, to things like the non-existent television aerial.

The first thing to be done was to work on the vineyard and prepare for the next harvest, when David had full intentions of bottling the wine. It needed fertilizer, soil testing, etc., and a general overhaul – bearing in mind that the harvest was only a few months off.

As much as possible was done that year which, with the help of the weather, resulted in a good harvest. The work in the vineyard continued for another three years, and I am pleased to say that it now looks a picture of health! Because of this concentration the house was almost completely neglected.

David and I worked together well [even though we are both stubborn and each want our own way], we both had one aim: getting Château Monplaisir put together. There was so much to do, the vineyards and the winery had been much improved and an oven to dry the plums had been installed in the plum building – yes, on that side things were looking up! The house was another story; my farmhouse was a palace compared to Château Monplaisir.

David had definitely bought it for location, location, location and nothing else! A very large van load of furniture from the UK had been delivered, put into the appropriate rooms and left, prior to David's arrival as he had to remain in Richmond to oversee the loading of the furniture.

When I arrived with a small group in 1998, we were made very welcome and invited into the sitting room to taste the wines of Monplaisir; I must be very honest and say this room was an absolute 'clutter'. No thought had been given to the placing of the furniture and there were several little tables covered with trinkets. Piles of books and newspapers were lying everywhere, as well as bookcases being absolutely crammed with more books and trinkets. This was the first day I gave much thought to Feng Shui!

Apart from the sitting room, there was a small kitchen and, from it, a door leading into a room which hadn't seen decoration for fifty years! The walls were black and there was shredded lino on the floor. This room was used for the washing machine and dryer, and everything else which couldn't be stored in the kitchen was to be found on the floor.

Beyond this room, there was yet another room which I was

unable to see clearly for several months as the small window had shutters and the electricity was in such a poor state it was dangerous. The walls were black from humidity. This was used to dump items which would never be used again but David didn't want to part with them!

The bedroom on the ground floor, facing over the valley, had a wooden floor, and the two large windows of three panes had been covered with plastic as some had cracks and the plastic gave a little protection. Unfortunately, it was a harbour for 'wee beasties' and one of the first things I did after moving in was to remove the plastic and have the cracked panes replaced. In the tower dressing room, leading from the bedroom, which was used as yet another storage area, humidity had started working on the cardboard boxes etc.

The room opposite had real problems: one wall was slowly disintegrating, the stones being dislodged by the dampness. At this time, I am able to explain, having done serious work with stone walls in the Dordogne, the walls of many of the older properties are built with the large stones found in the ground. The wall is actually two walls, inside and outside. In between, the space is filled with rubble and mud from the area; this mud has serious clay content and holds together beautifully. The downside is that clay soaks up moisture, and if the wall hasn't been properly sealed the clay will soak up the dampness and you will soon get evidence of this in the appearance of the walls! It is most important that the roof is well maintained, because if any part of the wall is exposed the rain will get into the wall and wash away the mud – in time demolishing the wall!

It was obvious that this is what had happened in the room we now use as a dining room. The wall was repaired and treated but looked a mess, so we decided to repair the plasterwork covering the wall by casing the lower half of all the walls in the room with pine – to match the floor, which had also just had the floorboards replaced. *Quelle difference!*

As I was still very much involved with my own work, the first thing I had to do was create an office as I had to accommodate all the furniture, books, files, etc. I had brought from Torquay.

The roof space above is quite large and it was in this area an office was made for me. You may find this difficult to believe, but although I moved in 2001, in 2005 I have not yet got my office properly laid out. There is so much to do everywhere else, the organising of my office is way down the list of priorities.

The access up to the office area was a fitted stepladder and, in time, climbing this became sore on the feet. My very good English friend Neil, who specialises in loft conversions, soon put this matter right. The first thing for me to do was to fax all the measurements he had requested – and they had to be exact. Not long after he arrived in his Land Rover full of wood and tools. Within a few days he had fitted a proper staircase and although very narrow as it had to be fitted into a cupboard running the full length of the wall – it has made such a difference.

Chapter 4

For Better — or for Worse

We went off to Antigua to get married in December 2001. No one was informed because if we had married in Edinburgh, from where we both originate, or London, then we should have had to arrange accommodation for friends from Edinburgh, London

and France. If we had married in France it would have meant a lot of organising, so we took the easy way out. We sent everyone a letter informing them of our deed and back came replies such as 'sneaky you' and several to say if they had known they would have come out to Antigua with us!

On our return, the car was waiting at the station, as arranged, and on getting into the vehicle we found a note saying, 'Ring Erick ASAP' [Erick, our estate manager and winemaker]. We thought immediately of robbery and as soon as we got home David called Erick.

Erick asked if we had had a look around the house, to which David replied, "No". Erick told him that he would be up right away. On putting down the phone, we started to look around the house and couldn't believe what we saw. The whole of the east wing had more or less been demolished by burst pipes. Water and damage everywhere!

Seemingly, whilst we were away enjoying the lovely sun, the Dordogne had a severe cold spell; the temperature had dropped to minus 15° and the water tank on the top of the tower had burst and flooded everything below.

Fortunately, our workers and friends had come in and emptied the rooms as best they could to prevent any more damage than necessary. Carpets, bed linen, curtains and all were thrown out of the windows. Nearly all the mattresses were absolutely ruined as by the time the damage was found they had been thoroughly soaked. Two new, huge fitted wardrobes had been soaked and just fallen apart and the clothes were ruined. The varnished wood floors were flooded and I never thought we would have been able to restore them.

One mattress had survived so we dragged that downstairs into the main part of the house. The sitting room was all right so there in a corner we put the mattress and that's where we slept for the following six months! Fortunately, this room possessed an excellent recently acquired wood-burning stove so we didn't have to freeze!

Now I know in the marriage vows you take your husband 'for better or for worse' but on our first night back at Château

Monplaisir, I felt I was going to experience the 'worse' before getting the 'better'.

The next morning the insurance expert arrived to say that 'things' had been organised and that work would start immediately. At this point, I want to praise the insurance system in France. There was absolutely no messing about; huge commercial blow dryers were brought into the house and strategically placed to dry out the damaged area. I said to David that we ought to go down and check my farmhouse, although I didn't expect any damage because a lot of work had been recently done in the house.

Don't you believe it...we opened the door and there was water everywhere. A similar thing had happened; the water tank had burst above the library and the furniture and books were ruined! Fortunately, it had happened the day before so we caught it in good time or the whole house could have been damaged. The Dordogne is a nightmare for insurance companies.

This catastrophe caused the start of the improvement work on the house sooner than we had anticipated and the first thing on my list was the kitchen.

The small kitchen was of no use really, except if you were a bachelor living on your own. There was extremely little working surface and cupboard space was limited. Beyond the kitchen there were two more rooms, which I would describe as the 'Black Holes of Calcutta'. These rooms were part of the original house and presumably the living room and bedroom of that time. The floors were cement, covered in lino and the walls had been papered about forty years ago. These had long turned yellow, and black in some places where the dampness had crept up the walls. The fireplace had long since fallen apart!

We made our way into the second room, and when we tried to put the light on David almost electrocuted himself by touching the bare wires! The floor in this part was cement and the small window hadn't been opened for years. Well, I thought, this is where we start.

To get rid of dampness is very difficult – especially when the outside wall is facing a hill which slopes towards your house! So the first thing to do was to build a terrace all along this wall and slope it slightly away from the house.

The majority of the earlier houses built in the region 'BBA' [before the British arrived] were of stone – both the outside and inside walls; between was filled with rubble and the clay soil of the region. The only problem was that if there is water near the foundations, this is sucked up by the rubble and the walls become damp. Damp courses were never used BBA. Chemicals had to be poured into two of the four walls.

Since building the terrace, we haven't had any problems and now, of course, we have a lovely outside dining room which is well used in the summer. The partitioning walls in the 'black holes' were knocked down and a proper kitchen was made.

The walls in the huge sitting room were covered in 1940s' dark green wallpaper and removing it took ages, but once off we were able to paint the walls in a lovely soft salmon colour, which is ideal for all the decorations such as paintings, photographs and souvenirs.

As the rest of the house had been badly damaged by the

flooding, the renovation was done by professionals but there was one room which had not been damaged and we took it upon ourselves to do the work. One of the walls had fallen apart and when David had bought the house he was told that it needed treatment – David had arranged for this to be done. To hide this part of the room, we decided to put metre-high pine boarding all around the room and paint the walls above white. It looked really nice for a few months, and then the second nightmare started…

We noticed that there was a fungus growing on the new wood; I couldn't believe it – dry rot! Immediately, we starting pulling the panelling from the walls and there we found more horrible evidence. On inspecting David's office [on the other side of the wall of the fireplace] there was a small patch of the fungus on that wall.

Drastic action was necessary; from all my experience in Dordogne restoration work I knew we had to find the source, so after ripping the panelling from the walls the next demolishing job was the floor! The fireplace had been built on the original floorboards and these were affected – hence it was creeping

through to David's office – so the fireplace had to be removed. Under the floorboards was nothing but earth, and the dry rot had lain dormant until we had replaced the old floorboards with new wood. It had been horrendous; taking up the rotten wood and replacing it with new pine. This was the big mistake. Dry rot can lie dormant for years but when it has a taste of new wood it goes mad – and this did. The fungus had spread everywhere, and when we took the new boarding down we found layers of the fungus creeping up the walls. I felt quite ill. Where had it come from?

We were soon to find out, because on further inspection we discovered that the floorboards had been fitted to a few beams resting in the soil beneath. That was it. I called in Philip, our local 'mason', and arranged for him to rip out every piece of wood and lay a cement floor, with a damp course, which would later be surfaced with tiles. "And while you're at it, Philip, do the same thing with the wooden floor in the room opposite – I don't want to see another wooden floor at ground level!"

Philip arrived and work was started without hesitation; all the wood was lifted and taken away to be burnt. A base was laid with the help of our workers, Erick and Selib, then lined, after which cement was poured in and a tiled floor replaced the wooden one. Such a relief!

I have really seen it all with floors in

Dordogne: from those where tiles have been laid straight onto the earth and when it rained, they floated about; to cement floors being laid straight onto earth and the floor being higher at one end of the room than the other; to my latest experience.

I have spent years involved in restoration work, and I honestly thought getting married and moving into Monplaisir, I could put this behind me, but no, it still goes on and I am now of the opinion I shall be building until I die!

With all the problems, it took about six months of living and eating in one room before we could move back into the bedroom. 'For better or for worse' rang out in my head!

Although I have had a property in the Dordogne for many years, I now felt that I had truly come to stay.

Chapter 5

Taking up Residency in France

Very few people moving to another country, such as those who take up residence in the Dordogne, realise what it involves and means to the people who live in the villages of the Dordogne when foreigners arrive on the scene. Some British make an effort to join in the community, others decide to live the colonial life and there are a few who try to 'lord it' over the locals. I have seen evidence of all three types over the thirty or more years of being part of the Dordogne. There seems to be confusion over the words 'peasants' and *paysants*.

When I came to the Dordogne with my ex-husband, we were the first British people in the area so we had no other choice than to live with the French and accept their very kind hospitality.

I heard rumours of unrest among the French people in the neighbourhood and also that in one or two of the small villages only a couple of the residents were French!

Yes, we may have lost the Hundred Years' War but we are certainly getting Aquitaine back – buying it back brick by brick.

The first time it was brought to my notice was on a visit to the local hairdresser. We were always able to have a little chat, although I spent most of my time finding 'Janet and John' words to translate into French. One day we discussed the number of Brits moving into the region; by this time Eymet was overflowing and Sigoules was taking the 'surplus'.

My hairdresser explained to me that she didn't mind all the ex-pats as it was good for business but she did object to them trying, and succeeding in some ways, to change the lifestyle of the villages. I agreed with her as I had not moved to the Dordogne to live the British colonial way of life. When the haircut had been completed I asked how much I owed her. Her reply was, "You can have the French price!"

Although I sympathise with the French, I feel they must accept that the Dordogne is what it is today because of the British and a few Dutch.

When I came here originally the place was desolate. The old houses were in poor condition and many of the barns were just falling apart. The furniture was either original or reproduction of the traditional type. There was very little 'flat pack'. There were very few French people who knew anything about 'do it yourself' and it took ages for the French to cotton on to this. They watched with curiosity and envy, in some ways, at the adeptness of the British handyman. As time went on they started to copy the Brits, so more and more of the type of DIY shops necessary for this work moved into Bergerac.

The British have done wonders with these old properties, which had been sold in order for the French to build 'Lego' houses with no character, being much smaller and therefore needing very little maintenance, but in the summer they are like hothouses. The sun belts in through the French doors which are fitted in nearly every room.

When I look around now and see the improvements done by the British, I often wonder how many French regret selling their ruined or unwanted properties as they did.

Now, most of us live together very happily and I enjoy being in the community. David and I make every effort to be 'communal'. We support the local *petanque* team and every year we offer the grounds of the chateau as a 'pit stop' for the annual September Le Raid cycle race. Last year there were nearly fifty who arrived, signed in, had a drink – some water, some wine – and a slice of apple or some nuts and continued on.

It was rather amusing for us because we supplied a glass of wine for each one, but the first half dozen – serious riders – didn't want to waste time so our vinous offer was refused. However, as the race continued, things changed.

In came those who didn't have a chance of winning and they would have a glass of wine. Then these pit stops became even longer as time was taken to admire my 1949 MG TD and even to spend a few minutes admiring the view from the chateau over the Dordogne Valley. It's always great fun and we look forward to the occasion each year.

In the summer, all the villages have fetes, jumble sales and the annual dinner dance. One particular summer, we were asked to help with the village fete by setting up a stand to sell our wines. It was explained that the organiser's father, who has one of the three vineyards in our village, was unable to participate as the family had to attend a wedding. The other vineyard had no interest so my dear husband said it was our duty to show willing and that we must support the village community. Although I could smell a rat, I made every effort to collect all the show pieces together to help out.

Without going into great detail, it was an absolute disaster. The organisation had been extremely poor – no publicity had been done and more or less no one had turned up! Needless to say, we didn't sell any bottles of wine. One glass was bought and we gave two away to elderly ladies who had bought a poke of chips and a sausage each at the nearby stand. Apart from the Maire and his assistant, there was almost no participation from any other person in the village.

It wasn't long before I gave my beloved David one of those looks – which said it all – and together we packed up everything and went home.

Later, when I complained to one of the Council about the poor organisation and participation of those who lived in the village he asked me if I would like to join the Council. "Not on your life," I said. Since then, there have been very few village 'get-togethers'.

To me, the people in this area have their priorities worked out properly. They are agricultural and work extremely hard during the week, but when it comes to Saturday and Sunday work is put in the background and eating plus family are put to the fore.

In the eighties, Saturday was the shopping day and entertainment took place in the evening. We had a couple of nightclubs – Château Monet Sully on the route to Mussidan and the other was out at Lalinde. One of the most popular was much further away in Libourne on the route to Bordeaux.

Sunday was a lazy day. Most families organised 'special' lunches and I was very fortunate to be involved but, I must add, I took my share of entertaining the locals by presenting a typical British meal on occasions. This was very well received – especially the English custard!

It's a lot different nowadays, Sunday lunches aren't as heavy – they are watching their regime and Saturday entertainment has become more sophisticated.

Airport of Bergerac

The Bergerac Airport is the 'Fastest Growing Airport in France' – and that's official.

When Ryanair was in its early years, I wrote to Mike O'Leary informing him that we had over 25 thousand ex pats in the South West and all were desperate for his type of service in the area. I was completely ignored.

Later, an acquaintance of mine started to push harder, even to the extent of getting Brits in the region of the Dordogne to sent postcards to Ryanair and Buzz which was in existence at the time.

In the end, Buzz agreed to take on the service and after many meetings with Bergerac Airport management came to an agreement. At that time Buzz was part of KLM who had as well as the airline, a transport service covering the whole of the UK.

It was the bright idea of one of the management of the newly formed BUZZ who suggested introducing a wine delivery service, ie door to door. All these transporters driving around Britain – sometimes with very little cargo - could be put to better use and therefore bring in more income for KLM.

Holidaymakers would be invited to visit the nominated chateaux of the Dordogne, order their wine and the producer would prepare and deliver the wine to the airport where Buzz staff was responsible for getting it back to the UK. Gosh! This was not only beneficial to Buzz but the boost it would give to the sales of Bergerac wines was quite unimaginable. As well as this, the reputation of Bergerac wines was bound to improve without doubt as very few of the quality wines are known in the UK. Such a dream......

Of course, this all took some time and a lot of planning and meetings – especially with Customs and Excise but after a few months, the way was clear to start. Order forms, waybills, labels, etc were printed and delivered to those châteaux that had been invited to join. By the end of the year, we had received all the necessary guidance and also a Buzz desk diary....

Bergerac (EGC) Airport Timetable

Flight No	Departure	Arrival	M	T	W	T	F	Sa	Su	Stop	A/C Change	Dates
Birmingham												
BE1982	14:05	15:05	M		W		F			-	-	19th October 2007 – 26th October 2007
BE1982	15:55	16:55							Su	-	-	21st October 2007 – 21st October 2007
Edinburgh												
BE1256	18:15	19:40						Sa		-	-	20th October 2007 – 27th October 2007
Exeter												
BE1794	13:05	13:40							Su	-	-	21st October 2007 – 21st October 2007
BE1794	13:20	13:55	M		W		F			-	-	19th October 2007 – 26th October 2007
BE1794	13:25	14:00	M				F			-	-	29th October 2007 – 28th March 2008
London Gatwick												
BE1549	18:15	18:55						Sa		-	-	20th October 2007 – 27th October 2007
Southampton												
BE1646	11:35	12:10							Su	-	-	21st October 2007 – 21st October 2007
BE1646	14:00	14:35	M	T	W	T	F			-	-	21st October 2007 – 26th October 2007
BE1646			M		W		F			-	-	29th October 2007 – 28th March 2008
BE1646								Sa		-	-	20th October 2007 – 27th October 2007
BE1646									Su	-	-	20th October 2007 – 28th March 2008

January and February passed and we were preparing for a summer of good sales. At the beginning of March, the bombshell came when we sat absolutely agog, unbelievably watching the news and hearing that KLM had sold BUZZ to Ryanair.

What was KLM thinking of? Most of the BUZZ operations were highly successful, in fact only two were ever mentioned to me as being poor.

Then blow number two came along when we learned that Ryanair had no intention of continuing with Bergerac and had agreed to run the service from Stansted to Bordeaux. We were just getting accustomed to having a service from Bergerac and it was all going to be taken away. That was until Bordeaux refused the sum per passenger offered by Ryanair as it was appallingly low compared to the passenger tax paid to Bordeaux by other airlines.

During this time, another airline had become interested in the UK Bergerac service – one of the staff at Bergerac Airport asked me if I had ever heard of Flybe. I said "No". But Flybe, part of British Midland, who have their administration offices in Exeter, had made a bid and it wasn't long before the management of Flybe paid a visit to Chateau Monplaisir – including a tasty lunch. Here we go again – but this time, wine sales weren't included.

At first I thought Southampton a bit out of the way for London but during the management visit it was explained that this airport is most convenient for London as trains run every half hour from Waterloo – which was quite attractive. What was ALSO mentioned was the cost of the rail fare from London to Southampton – which is quite a hefty sum!

So it was confirmed, there would be a service from Bergerac to Southampton. Then not long after, we heard that Ryanair was unable to persuade Bordeaux to lower their rate of tax and because of this, they were reconsidering Bergerac.

The main problem at Bergerac was the runway which was in no way long enough, wide enough or constructed well enough to take the larger planes of Ryanair. After a series of meetings to discuss this, the owner of Bergerac Airport agreed to do the work and within the dictated period of just a few weeks. I have never seen things happen so quickly in France! The airport was operational within the period demanded by Ryanair.

It was all happening – the little airport which had a rather poor service to Paris and WAS mainly used BY the parachute club and FOR short sightseeing trips around Bergerac – had become 'International'. We couldn't believe it! It is a privately owned airport – which may explain the speed in which the work was completed.

As time went on, more destinations were introduced by the two airlines, Bristol, Liverpool and Norwich – to name just a few... In fact, 2007 brought in flights to and from Edinburgh and Gatwick to join the most recent, Exeter.

In 2004 there were 200,000 passengers, in 2005, roughly 300,000 passengers and in 2006, this increased to 400,000 passengers. The number of passengers using the airport in

2007 will be quite interesting to see.

Very little was done to the concourse and that was mainly because of disagreement with the Bergerac Council, *Chambre de Commerce* and the owner – money dictates. When it all first started to happen, the airport requested financial help from the public and from the councils of the towns which were going to benefit from this airport, ie other towns in the Dordogne and beyond. Let's face it, getting to Bordeaux airport by road from this side is HELL!

The route is only about 50 miles but through many villages with a speed restriction of about 30 miles per hour – thus making the journey not only unnecessarily long but also most frustrating as you are held up continually with traffic, tractors and so on.....
Once you have made your way to the east side of Bordeaux, you have then to cross the Garonne River and this can take an hour or more – simply because of the incessant blockages of traffic.

It was planned several years ago to have an autoroute from Bordeaux to Bergerac and then on to Perigueux. The vineyard producers from both Pomerol and St Emilion fought against it as it would have meant taking the road through these prestige vineyards. Because of this, the autoroute was re-planned; it runs from Bordeaux to Libourne but instead of continuing to Bergerac, from Libourne it now turns north to Perigueux – thus leaving a very poor road between Libourne and Bergerac through several villages where the speed has to be reduced to 50 km per hour. This causes havoc – especially at the weekends when you have all the commuter traffic.

With the recent build up of Bergerac - airport, increased number of visitors, industry, etc there is now even more traffic on this road and if I was the owner of a crystal ball I would predict in the not too distant future, an autoroute will have to be put in place between Bergerac and Libourne.

A few years ago, this privately owned airport had a service to Paris two or three times a day – which was so expensive that it was cheaper to go by train! The only other activity was a parachuting club – which is one of the best in France. There is talk at the moment of moving this club to Perigueux as the flight programme to and from the UK is expanding rapidly and this is causing a situation where accidents could happen. The members of the Club are not very happy about this move.

Very little has been done to cope with the number of passengers now using the airport. I have been told that there is an expansion programme and seen the plan of the future airport but have seen no evidence of this work. There seems to be a lot of argument over who is going to pay for it all as the airport is now used by those living well outside of Bergerac, ie St Emilion, Agen and Sarlat and the commune of Bergerac feels that other communes should help financially with the work that has to be done.

Of course, while this argument continued, the airport was losing an incredible amount of money as you could park free – and for as long as you liked. This was encouraging people to leave their cars for months on end and up until the opening of the new car park, we had hundreds of cars spread all over the fields around the airport!

This means that British homeowners in the area could travel as they pleased from Liverpool, Nottingham, Leeds, Birmingham, Bristol, Exeter, Southampton and London to Bergerac, pick up their car and drive home!!!!!!! You were even advised by the 'grapevine' to keep a charger in the car……….

I should imagine that the parking charges which could have been accumulated over the last three years would have just about paid for some of the expansion work.

Don't be surprised on your arrival at the airport for the first time – the baggage reclamation system is primitive. From the plane to the building is exceptionally well organised but once the hatch to receive the baggage is opened the fun begins. There is no carousel – there is a conveyor length of runners and your baggage is literally thrown on to that by the baggage handler and it is the job of the passengers nearest this belt to push the baggage down its length. If you are not near the belt, your baggage arrives in the pile at the end and if the plane is packed as is normally the way, it's murder trying to get through the crowds in the small area, collect your luggage and then return through the crowd to get to the custom gate – which is a little wider than an ordinary door.

[During my travels around the world, there is only one baggage room worse and that is Antigua which I shall be writing about in my next book.]

On our return from a winter holiday, we arrived at Bergerac at one of the busiest times – a few days before Christmas. The plane was packed and it took an age to retrieve our baggage and make our way to passport control. Everyone was questioned at the gate – especially those in weird dress or with bizarre haircuts. By the time we got to the officer I was exhausted and suggested that they should widen the door and have two lines – one for residents and the other for visitors. On occasions there are two officers now.

The airport Restaurant was yet another problem and a definite case for Gordon Ramsey's Hell's Kitchen treatment – but I don't think I could take the….language!

You were continually hearing all these reports of how Bergerac Airport was desperate for financial help in order to expand its airport.

Apart from the fact that they are losing thousands of euros by not charging for parking as people left their cars for up to six months – free of charge; there was also another waste of money and that was an inadequate restaurant which is not big enough to cope with the lunchtime traffic which has been created by three of the flights to the UK leaving at around 2.30 pm.

On one particular trip, we decided that it would be a good idea to leave earlier for the airport for our journey to Southampton on Flybe which left the airport at 2.45 pm – thus being able to have a leisurely lunch after checking in at the Airport restaurant – what came to pass was unbelievable.

We were too early for the check in, so decided to go straight to the restaurant. It was packed, but fortunately one table in the centre was available. We sat down just after 12 noon and about thirty-five minutes passed before the waitress came to take our order.

Over the public speaking system, it was announced by an English speaking woman that the 'check in' for Southampton was open. It was later announced by the same person in French - and like many others, proving to all their fluency in the French language she reeled off the message at such a speed that no one could understand the French as there was no pronunciation of each word!

The same thing happens on the flight and I often wonder if the French people think that the British Education is incapable of teaching proper French.....

At one fifteen, the omelette had still not been brought to the table and by that time several people had cancelled their orders and left the restaurant. We were told that we had to be in the airport by one thirty, so at one twenty-five, I went to the staff of the restaurant and explained that we would be leaving as well!

With that, the omelette was brought out immediately and I proceeded to eat – only to start choking as I was rushing the food down my throat [in general I am a very slow eater]. My husband had to rush for extra water for me.

Everyone was moaning about the service as they left but one lady said that this was the worst she had ever seen and that on the majority of times she had been to the restaurant the service had been reasonably good.

Well, what more can I say, other than advise you never to plan a quick meal at the airport restaurant?

It wasn't long after that 'war' broke out at the airport restaurant. Seemingly, the Lease had run out and the holders, mother and daughter, wanted it renewed. This was natural, bearing in mind the potential of the restaurant with such a fast growing expansion programme.

The local papers reported the support given to the leaseholders and how they refused to leave the premises. Hundreds of British passengers signed a petition – it was getting out of hand.

Large investment would be required to bring the restaurant into line with the growth of the airport and the Chamber Of

Commerce refused to renew the Lease and eventually took over the premises.

Some time ago I met my friend Monsieur Rolland who manages one of the top restaurants in Bergerac; he told me of his intention to take over the airport restaurant – this was music to my ears as we spend a lot of time at the airport due to the travelling we have to do......... The thought of sitting down to a well prepared meal whilst waiting for the flight certainly appeals to me! At the moment, there is very little comfort offered to waiting passengers.

It wasn't long before it was confirmed that the restaurant would come under new management.

During the summer, flights to the UK start from about nine o'clock and the last one goes out at ten thirty in the evening and this new restaurant is going to make a fantastic difference.

With redecoration and refurbishing, I should imagine the restaurant will attract not only the passengers but also aviation enthusiasts who will enjoy eating well and watching the activities of the airport which includes private and military take offs and landings.

Not only is Monsieur Rolland an excellent, experienced chef – who has been honoured by President Chirac for his work in the industry – but also a well known character of the *vieux quartier* business of Bergerac. My own opinion – and here I go again – is that this 'character' will be sadly missed.

On recent visits to the Airport I saw quite a change; the restaurant has been refurnished [ie more chairs and tables both inside and out] but not yet redecorated. I got the impression that staff were more organised and service is certainly better. Management also seem to be coping well with the busy periods when two or three flights are departing at the same time.

Chapter 6

Women in Wine in Bergerac

There have always been women in Bergerac wine production – even from my early days!

Whenever I think of women in wine, my mind turns to those in Champagne who made such a success of their work. Louise Pommery who did so much for the marketing of Champagne. Then the very important Veuve Cliquot; if it wasn't for her we may well have still been drinking champagne from tall, hollow-stemmed glasses which held the sediment from the second fermentation. It was only when Madame Cliquot discovered how to get the sediment to the neck of the bottle then dispersing it by *dégorgement* that we had a clear wine. This was done by freezing the sediment gathered and then removing the temporary screw cap under pressure – the frozen sediment burst out of the bottle. The *méthode champenoise* could then be completed.

No woman in Bergerac has attained such glory, but two or three ladies stand out very much to the fore when I think of the eighties and the ladies from the Pécharmant region. At that time Bergerac wines were very poorly regarded. The only red wine worth drinking was from Pécharmant and women were very much involved with this production.

Mme Roche Veuve came into my life when her grandchildren had started to learn English at school. She had been left widowed and had to manage the vineyard with little help as, I'm not sure how long before this her husband had died, but I do know that the son was still working in the tobacco laboratories in Bergerac and when he wasn't doing that he was helping his mother look after the vineyards. In fact, the whole family was involved. [It should be noted that Bergerac was a very important centre for tobacco up until just recently. The laboratories opposite the Bergerac 'Powdery' on the road to Sarlat employed many people, and Monsieur Roche Junior had quite a senior position so it must have been very difficult for him.] The whole family pulled together to keep the vineyards in order. The wines from the Roche family are regarded as some of the best Pécharmants.

My 'side job' was to arrange exchanges of students wanting to learn English which meant me accompanying the children to the UK, being on hand during their stay and returning to France with them. It was a very personal service, offered simply because I had watched foreign students coming to Devon in groups and being accommodated by families but, unfortunately, the 'groups' ended up together in the evenings so any good work which had been done in the language schools during the day was lost during the evening. Such a waste, I thought, knowing the problems I had arriving in France without a word of French!

Mme de Corbiac was another prominent woman in wine who put an awful lot of effort into marketing her wines, during a very difficult period. I spoke with her on a couple of occasions and my impression was that she was a very determined woman, with good reason for being determined! Château Corbiac has been in the family for generations and historically is one of the most important, but keeping it in the family means great sacrifices, unless you have a family like the Rothschilds where continual investment is no problem!

Owning a vineyard can be equated to owning a reservoir and instead of putting water into it you throw in money which the land soaks up!

It must be a great relief to her having a son, Antoine, who is now fully trained in many facets of the wine business. He has been able enough to take over and relieve his parents of some of the responsibilities. There is more about him later in the book.

Then there was the Comtesse de Saint-Exupéry who was very much involved in the wine production of Château Tiregand. She and Mme Roche were two of the producers of the very tannic Pécharmant which by the time the tannins softened the fruit had almost disappeared! I always remember on one of my visits to Tiregand with her son, François-Xavier, when we did a radio show together, he told me that since that time the method of fermentation had been modernised but his mother still had the last word in the final blending of the wines.

The Exupéry family are cousins of the same family in the Medoc – famous winemakers for many generations. I have known François-Xavier for many years but met his brother only once – he spends his time working very hard behind the scenes.

The Exupéry family are in a similar situation to the Corbiacs. Both have beautiful historical chateaux which should really have been publicly supported to restore them as nearly as possible to their original state. Unfortunately, Château de Tiregand has been more or less completely destroyed by termites. Such a waste.

I remember doing some research into the Château de Duras – another which had been left to ruin. I was told that there are so many chateaux in France and there is an organisation similar to English Heritage, but they can't cope with all the restoration work!

In the nineties more women came to the fore. Patricia Atkinson, with help from both French and English wine producers and ex pats [who help to hand-pick the grapes for her], started producing a sweet wine of Saussignac. At that time she had a small vineyard of about four hectares. Later, one of her French neighbours, a producer nearby, offered her his vineyard. She then had to find financial help and investors joined her to become shareholders in the business which enabled the purchase and running of the larger vineyard.

Then came Marianne Mallard of Château Pique Segue. She was the 'darling' of some of my male passengers. Bernard, who described her as "dynamic" and just dwelled on every word she uttered – in fact, he may have come twice to the Dordogne with me on tour and I'm sure it was for 'just another glimpse!' Her wines are very good, especially the rosé – absolutely delightful. Marianne's family home is in Paris but she is a regular visitor to Ste Foy La Grande where she keeps a careful eye on her vineyard in the Montravel region of Bergerac.

I think I made about three visits to her winery, and on the last occasion I had the pleasure of catching up with the oenologist who had actually introduced me to Bergerac wines as he was the oenologist that had conducted the courses for vignerons at the Maison du Vin in Bergerac – when I first started on the long trail of wine knowledge. I still see Marianne once in a while at the London Wine Shows and her wines are even better.

It was in 1997, just after David had completed the purchase of Château Monplaisir, that Olivia Noonan and her husband visited Gageac. They were also interested in Château Monplaisir but, of course, it had just been sold and they later purchased Château Masburel.

I have never thought that there was anyone as mad as me when it comes to restoring properties. Years and years of hard work, spending your time in stone and cement; having to give up such luxuries as time to spend on yourself, the odd manicure, hairdresser visits, even the occasional facial or massage, being dressed in a feminine way instead of the continual shorts/jeans and a T-shirt, cut hands and bruised legs. Just recently, I met someone similar – Olivia.

I first met her a few years ago at one of the London Wine Fairs; actually I popped over to the Bergerac stand to have a chat

with Marianne who had informed me that she would be there for two of the days of the exhibition.

Olivia was already creating her place in the wine world and I admired her effort. She was popping up at many of the events I attended, representing the press. My first thought was the cost of her being present at all these shows.

Recently, when I visited Château de Masburel this was one of the first questions I asked her: Had she gained from such a large investment in publicity? Then after looking around the office, at paper cuttings and wine medal award certificates, I had the answer.

As we talked and walked around the winery, she explained the work that had been done since she and her husband took over the property in 1997. It wasn't only coping with the mud floors in the winery but also renovating the outhouses, building partition walls to make areas for stockage, showroom and an office.

There has been a tremendous amount of work done on the house and the gardens during the last eight years but I could tell that Olivia was pleased with her endeavours. Now she is able to concentrate, with her team, on making top quality wine. She confided in me that her dream is to be the producer of the 'Petrus' of Bergerac. On reflection, I feel that if her wish was modified to becoming one of the Grand Cru producers of Bergerac: this would be a possibility.

Last, but not least, is the youngest member of Women in Wine in Bergerac. Her name is Katarina and she produces wine at Château K. There is a lot written about her further on in the book. She is a winemaker I shall be keeping my eye on; her wines are extremely promising.

Chapter 7

Gastronomy in The Dordogne

There is no doubt that your interest in food will increase if you come to live or holiday in the Dordogne – even if you had no interest in food before – but I should add that I think that everyone I know and have met who has come to the Dordogne to live or even to holiday has an interest in food.

Apart from it being cheaper to eat here there is an abundance of fresh food in the supermarkets. For example, I am a great salad eater and I have a choice of at least six different types of lettuce and three of tomatoes – and that is all the year round. There is even a bigger selection in the summer!

I am also a great collector of cook books but whenever I feel lazy all I have to do is go out with an open mind into the markets – or supermarkets - of the Dordogne where the delights are displayed beautifully before you and you can make an instant decision on the menu for the day! It's so simple here.

People in France are inclined to shop more often; the old fashioned daily shopping has now died out but there are still many who buy from the supermarket two or three times a week.

The weekly markets and the village shops have not been neglected either. Fresh meat with personal advice on cooking – topped up with a very nice bone for the dog - is appreciated.

These markets offer an array of locally grown fruit and veg, nuts and prunes as well as those special little cheeses. There is always fish including a good selection of shell fish.

There is still a tendency for the older people to buy chickens which are killed before your very eyes – you could not get them much fresher than that! I suppose the threat of bird flu has restricted that because even my favourite producer can no longer allow the chicken out to enjoy freedom and fresh air. There is a new law in France which has curtailed chickens leaving the batteries to ensure that they don't come in contact with migrating birds.

A lot of village ladies have two kitchens – one for every day cooking and the other for conserving – because it is not only duck and chicken they prepare in jars and cans; you can add pork, vegetables and fruit. In the kitchen where they prepare the conserves you will find canning machinery, sterilizers and all sorts of tools required for this work. I was absolutely amazed when I witnessed the first events – all this work…. done in the kitchen!

The Dordogne is a gastronomic region of France and if you come over here on holiday – or to take up residence don't expect not to put on weight!

I enjoy cooking very much – especially when you have everything to hand as is the case in the Dordogne. I don't profess to being a great chef – because I'm not but I have always enjoyed giving lunches and dinner parties and I honestly believe if you have a deep interest in wine as I have – it only follows on that that interest carries on through to food.

In the following chapters, I am going to give you some idea of what happens in my culinary life.

Chapter 8

Dordogne Produce

Duck

The duck must be the most popular poultry in France – and every part of the bird is used in one way and another.

It is very sad that the recent world news indicates that the poultry industry of France may be significantly affected by recent developments.

I for one don't intend to give up eating poultry unless there is confirmation that this illness could spread to adults.

Rabbit

I don't think the British have ever recovered from the rabbit illness of myxomatosis. Unfortunately, I don't know much about it so I can't understand why the continuation of fear still remains. From what I gather it IS a terrible disease.

When I first started taking wine tours to the Dordogne the best winery visit was to Chateau La Meyrand Lacombe. The family were always very pleased to have us and Madame Lorenzon made the most superb *paté de lapin*. I could thoroughly recommend it to the passengers because I knew exactly how the rabbits were reared. Madame Lorenzon had a little house for them. They were well fed and had loads of room to move around. Seeing the little house completely reversed my opinion of not eating rabbit because of disease. Her speciality was in the production of the most wonderful patés - as well as *foie gras*, *confit de canard*, *magret* and so on from her ducks.

Of course, she couldn't manage all the work involved so several of her friends would come and stay for a few days – and they would work from sun up to sun down then wile away the evening with an excellent dinner which had been prepared well in advance of the busy period by Madame Lorenzon. This was accompanied with their own wine and perhaps a *soupçon* or two of prunes in *l'eau de vie* with their coffee. Ladies liked to soak a lump of sugar in the liqueur. I don't know if you are familiar with this type of *digestif*, but after your coffee, when the cup is still warm you add the prune and some of the liqueur. It's quite an experience and you can read more about it in the chapter on prunes.

Before taking the group on tour I always asked to see the menus proposed by the hotel and on one particular occasion, I noticed that rabbit with a *mustard de Dijon* sauce was in the selection. Very bravely, I asked it to be included in one of our evening menus.

As we drove south through France to the Dordogne, I discussed the food we would be having on tour. This was a regular thing; I am of the opinion that when you visit a wine region, you must have a chance to taste as much of the local food as possible. When we got the plate *"lapin avec la sauce moutarde de Dijon"*, I read it out and waited for the response – there was silence! So I slowly and quite definitely said that if there was anyone who was against eating rabbit – there was no problem as I had pre-warned the chef of the British reluctance to eat rabbit. With that – there was a much more relaxed aura on the coach. Of course, I knew that at the first opportunity there would be one or two who come to me with some sort of excuse – other than the obvious which was "we've never touched rabbit since the dreadful disease which swept the rabbit world many years ago".

Another favourite rabbit recipe for me is *'lapin a l'oignon'*. Here you take one rabbit and at least a kilo of onions and cook very slowly. We had it just recently with Brussels sprouts and cooked small lettuce hearts – delicious.

Also, have you ever had rabbit with prunes and red wine? A perfect recipe for Château Monplaisir.

Chicken

When I first came to France, I had great difficulty finding a fresh chicken in the shops so I asked my French neighbour if she could get one for me. It was a scraggy thing, deep yellow in colour and it cost a lot…….

It was then that I found out there are two ways to feed a chicken – either by maize or barley. The ones fed on maize are the yellow ones and even nowadays locals insist on eating these.

There is no problem buying chicken today. We are very fortunate in Bergerac because, and I know it's 'battery chicken style', but we have a very good producer called' Blaison d'Or' and their chickens arrive in the supermarket fresh and of good quality.

However contrary to local tastes, I prefer the white chicken which I marinade in Bergerac Sec with a whole sliced lemon, onions, salt, pepper and garlic.

Pork

Let's now have a look at conserving Pork.

Madame Prevôt was more into pork and vegetables although she also kept poultry. As well as their house, they own the little ruin next door to my farmhouse and one day she invited me in to watch her prepare the cured ham. There, in this ruin, were freezers and shelves all around the walls packed with kiln jars of vegetables, fruit, patés, confit and many other conserves! Tesco's – eat your heart out!

On seeing all of this, I mumbled something like "you'll never be able to eat all this – why have you got so much?" "Well", she said, "we may have another war and I want to make sure we can last for ten years!" I was speechless and continued to watch her peppering and salting the ham.

The ham is left in salt for about forty days. After this, the salt is cleared off and the skin is cleaned with *'eau de vie'* [this stops the mice attacking the ham]! It is then covered in black pepper.

For months, Porky the pig lay on straw in a little pig house attached to the main house. He was so big and fat but I must say, always very, very clean.

We always knew when it was going to start – in February - and Monsieur le Boucherie would arrive in his little van. The pig was slaughtered and it was a case of "Let work commence".

Madame Prevôt and her friends got cracking and every part of the pig was used and for sure, I knew that later in the evening a huge pan of black pudding soup would arrive at my door. It sounds quite dreadful, but by the time I had finished 'doing things' with it we had a very tasty bowl of soup. This soup is made with black pudding and vegetables – lots of cabbage and is very, very greasy, so the first job was to cool it down and place it in the fridge overnight. The next morning I removed the fat and put the vegetables in the machine – gave them a zzzzzzz and returned the mixture to the soup. Believe it or not, the soup was very good.

For several days after, Madame Prevôt was busy making paté, sausages and bagging cuts of pork for the freezer.

This isn't the end of the 'pork' story. It is the season and to celebrate the month of the Pig we do that by having a pork lunch in the village hall. It starts off with a kir, then crudités, hot black pudding and mustard, sausages, pork chops with conserved green beans, pieces of cheese and ice cream with coffee to finish. The wine flows from all the vineyards around the village and lots of stories are told over the white paper tablecloth. How about that?

Lamb

Lamb is also a popular dish but not always to the taste of the British. The French have it underdone and serve it with green flageolet beans which have been seasoned and had garlic and bits of ham added to them.

The British are always asking me what the French do with their vegetables as most meat and fish dishes are served with only one vegetable. This is very true and the following gives you an example.

We had some English people coming to lunch and I decided to roast a leg of lamb. My lady who gives me a hand with the cooking asked me to buy three large cans of flageolet – or a large sack of fresh ones [in season] and she would prepare them. My dear husband was most upset when he heard this news. "I want roast potatoes with the lamb!"

Now I was completely responsible for this dilemma because I know full well that the French always serve slices of pink lamb on a bed of flageolet – so the night before, I peeled and cut some potatoes and surreptitiously included them in the preparation for the lunch. Funny looks were given at the sight of the potatoes – but I said to my dear French friend, "You know, the British compare a main course without potatoes like the French would compare a meal without bread….and wine – like a day without sunshine! " A smile curled on her lips.

I am not enamoured by this dish; I suppose I would appreciate it more if it was served on a hot plate and we started eating immediately but the system seems to be that they slice up the lamb, put it on your cold plate and then you have to wait until you are served the flageolet – and this may take some time!!!! Barbequing a lamb in the summer is a great occasion. This is usually a communal meal and is called the '*meschio*'.

Last summer we were invited to one held in the woods just north of Le Fleix on the Dordogne. It was an exceptional occasion – they were celebrating the 40th anniversary of this picnic lunch in the woods.

We started off with a Kir – or was it two? We chatted away with everyone nearby – introducing ourselves and finding out about them. At our table we had a chap and his brother – both with their families and they work in the local stainless steel business – making vats for the wineries. One brother was known to us because about a year ago he came to ask permission to shoot the pigeons on our land. We had no objections about this and later we received two jars of Confit of Pigeon. Actually, it was the first time I had tasted pigeon and I enjoyed the dish – very much like quail.

The wife of one is French Canadian. She had spent most of her young life in Quebec and decided to return to her homeland. She wasn't the only one who had lived in Canada; Nadine sitting opposite with Maurice, left the Dordogne about thirty years ago and settled well in Montreal. She had a little hairdressing business as well as a small restaurant which I think they opened in the evenings. Everything went well until a few years ago when her husband died and Nadine's mother [who is now ninety two and still living in the Dordogne] asked her to come home. Nadine did – but I am not sure whether or not she did the right thing.

Life in the Dordogne has changed – but not that much – whereas Montreal is very modern and beautiful and I feel Nadine may have been better staying there because I can tell when she talks about it - which is often......

There is usually a huge gap between courses and the woodland lunch was no different. We started with soup and that was followed by a salad *Piedmontese*.

[This is what you would call a very filling salad, of potatoes, pieces of ham and boiled eggs which have been chopped into four or six pieces – then the whole dish is covered in a thick dressing.]

Much later, the lamb arrived at the tables - huge chunks of it – there had been four lambs on the spits being turned since early morning.......

We always take our dog, Ravi, with us to restaurants and picnics. The French are not like the British – the dogs are welcomed and usually a bowl of water is brought out to them. Ravi lies asleep under the table until it is time to leave, though he is usually alert for a bone even if often disappointed.

This occasion was quite different – Ravi thought it was Christmas! Mammoth lamb bones kept coming over – he was overwhelmed! It was all too much…… Ravi couldn't cope with it and in the end, we put the bones in a spare plastic carrier and Ravi lived in ecstasy for the next week or so.

It is normal to carry spare plastic bags because we were told that you can often find *cèpes* in the woods – but it wasn't to be. We were told later that this particular year wasn't 'a good *cèpes* year'.

The lunch finished with Camembert cheese, ice cream for the dessert and coffee.

The music continued to play; we said our 'thank you' to everyone and left immediately after. Being knowledgeable about life in the Dordogne, I know that this is the best thing to do or else………. They continued to drink and talk until about seven o'clock, and then the brothers invited everyone back to their house for dinner – *Confit de Pigeon*. Maurice and Nadine told us the following day that they didn't get home until three o'clock in the morning – I rest my case……

Beef

Beef has been the great favourite in cafes and restaurants in France. Steak-Frites is always available and at a very reasonable price. The state of the steak varies – sometimes you are lucky, other times you can get a fatty piece of beef which has just touched the frying pan and doesn't look very inviting…….

When it comes to roast beef, I have to give the French credit but that is because I like beef not too well done. For an average roast for 4-6 people the beef is put into a very hot oven for 20-30 mins, after which the meat is taken out and left to rest.

Garlic

Garlic has an interesting history to tell.

In the First World War, France couldn't produce enough for the British Forces who used it in the battle field hospitals in great quantities – not for cooking but to help in the treatment of gangrene and other associated nasties suffered by the troops of that time. It is used by village people nowadays to treat colds – a bit smelly used in this way!

In France, garlic is used in everyday cooking – and lots of it – and we don't mind our breath smelling of it as the French are sometimes accused of……. After all, it is not noticed because nearly everyone has garlic.

Henry II of France had a favourite recipe which included one chicken and two kilos of garlic! A couple of cloves are as much as I would add.

Grilled meat is truly enhanced with chopped parsley and garlic. The French prepare this in bulk and keep it in a jar in the fridge for the weekly use.

My favourite recipe is Garlic soup which is listed with other recipes further in the book.

Green Figs

Green Figs are also in abundance here - I have two trees in the garden. I had never eaten a fig before I came to France and now I wait patiently for them to ripen. I just take a few from the tree and chop and mix them with some *fromage frais* – delicious for breakfast. Last year I tried Jamie Oliver's excellent green fig salad, he has a fancy name for it which I can't remember – something like 'sexy salad'………

Walnuts

Walnuts are one of the first things I must talk about – it is 'the tree of the Dordogne' and whenever I am in UK and I visit a supermarket and see walnuts – I am 'jetted' right back to Bergerac. It is one of the treasures of the Dordogne and walnut trees can be found everywhere.

Unfortunately, this tree comes out of the ground much easier than the majority of other trees and sometimes this can happen during a storm – of which we have many in the Dordogne.

At one time furniture was made from walnut wood. I have a wardrobe made from one tree – there isn't a nail in the whole piece of furniture. It was common practice to give a boy at his christening a walnut tree which had been cut down and prepared for the long drying period. The idea being that by the time he got married, the wood would be well seasoned and ready for making furniture. 'Flat packs' didn't become popular until the 80s; people still preferred to have reproduction furniture and wood had to be around twenty years of age for this work.

Of course, walnut wood wasn't the only wood in the region, oak was plentiful and also cherry – a wood which I adore because of the red grain running through it.

There were so many lovely pieces of furniture made in walnut but the most outstanding were the different styles of tall wardrobes. As mentioned in the Chateau de Monbazillac chapter, there are fine examples of these beautiful pieces of furniture to be seen in the rooms of the chateau.

When the French started selling up their old farmhouses to build a more convenient type of 'Lego' style house, they found that a lot of the furniture they possessed would not fit into the new type of house – so they sold it! During the period of these old houses being sold, you were able to buy such items for a reasonable price – but now, items such as these are extremely difficult to find and when you do – the price is enormous!

There aren't nearly as many walnut trees nowadays and the wood isn't used for furniture as much as it was in the past, so the beautiful pieces which you can find in the converted barns around the area are a good reminder of our heritage.

At one time nearly every household had a walnut tree and this was the property of the woman of the house. In the autumn, she would take the walnuts to market to sell and the money she collected was her pocket money.

Aside from furniture, walnuts are used in several ways – first and foremost we have walnut oil, but they are also used for making liqueurs. You take the walnut from the tree when it has still got its green jacket which you prick all over with a large needle. After this, put them in a jar and cover with *l'eau de vie* and in time you will have a dark brown liqueur.

Additionally they are used for wood staining. Most of us have suffered from stains on natural wood at one time or another and, not in all cases, but in the majority, a walnut can help. You prepare the walnut in the same way as you would for the liqueur then you rub the green skin into the stain [make sure that you are wearing protective gloves to prevent your fingers from being stained as well!].

The walnut tree is a beautiful tree – and offers so much but unfortunately it doesn't age as well as others. Life is often cut short because of its root structure. The roots of other trees spread outwards – taking a good grip of the ground, but with the walnut tree the roots go straight down thus it comes out of the ground much easier than the majority of other trees and sometimes this can happen during a freak storm – of which we have many in the Dordogne.

This happened to me a few years ago. I had a beautiful old walnut tree in the garden. I remember one particular year, after a long illness, my Aunt Helen came down for a holiday, I put a sun bed under the tree and there she sat eating the cherries from the nearby cherry tree. The following year in the month of August, we had a freak Tornado and it lifted the walnut tree out of the ground and literally threw it over the cherry tree. It is very strange that since then, in the autumn, you will find a ring of edible mushrooms growing where the cherry tree once stood.

Chestnuts

Chestnuts are also plentiful and we use them a lot in cooking – in masses of different dishes – from soup to dessert. My favourite soup recipe can be found later in the book.

Prunes

With an orchard of 1500 plum trees, you will not be surprised to learn that I am always looking for recipes which include prunes!

A list of the following dishes – some already mentioned – is regularly on my menu.

Prunes rolled in streaky bacon – as a titbit with the aperitif
Cockaleekie soup
Rabbit with prunes
Roast pork stuffed with prunes
Fillet of pork with prunes
Clafouti with prunes
Fromage frais with prunes

A Different Type of Lettuce

Before the machines were brought into the vineyard to pick the grapes, the space between the rows of vines was much wider than today and in the spaces you would find plum trees, apples and pears as well as little salad gardens with lettuce, cucumbers, onions and tomatoes. As well as the things we planted, you could find wild onions and mache – a miniature type of lettuce.

I remember staying overnight in a plush hotel in Belgium en route to the vineyards of the Mosel and Rhine; dinner was superb. The first course was introduced as 'something very special' – it was warm cheese set on a bed of mache. The waiter explained that the mache had been flown in from France.

Mache is another type of lettuce with tiny leaves and lots of flavour. When my friend Simone visited for lunch during the summer season we always spent a little time walking through the vineyards – just to see what we could find. A lot of the time was spent digging up some mache, we then took it back to the farmhouse to wash and dry it. If the latter was done properly, the mache would last the week.

Drying lettuce and the like is taken quite seriously, as it is used every day in the menu. To save you from having to give time each day to preparing lettuce, the French have a slightly different way of preparing it.

It is washed in a sink full of water then transferred to the lettuce spinner when you spin it a couple of times. After this you put the lettuce into a clean drying cloth which will absorb any water which may remain. The lettuce is then put into a plastic bag which can be sealed and opened as necessary. In this way, you can keep the lettuce for nearly a week – in a 'ready to use' way.

Mushrooms

I have always enjoyed mushrooms and think of the time, when quite young, my uncle would take us out to dinner at the Elizabeth Grill in Edinburgh. His first plate was always mushrooms which had been cooked in butter and seasoning and served on freshly toasted bread!

This was quite new to me as at home the only time we had mushrooms or should I say, a mushroom, was with bacon and egg..........

My mushroom knowledge has increased tremendously since coming to France. I didn't read about them in books – too risky, you could still make mistakes. Instead, I have spent many years joining in with the locals and I listened to all I was told and watched very carefully how to pick mushrooms.

Cèpes

The locals are great *Cèpes* pickers and there is a lot of excitement and talk about the mushrooms when they are in the woods.

The best time to collect *cèpes* is very early in the morning. My friends Simone and Jean-Loup would get up as early as four o'clock and come back with enough to see them through the winter.

Cèpes are to be found at the base of the oak tree and come out twice a year – always after a huge deluge of rain. You can find them in June but they are smaller then and not nearly as tasty as the gigantic ones which appear in October – definitely the best month. Some of these are as big as a dinner plate and between one and two inches thick – perhaps even bigger. They are very expensive to buy in the market or shops and accompanied with dishes in a restaurant can add a hefty amount to your bill.

I dread to think of the price in the UK. I have read of London restaurateurs going down as far as Devon to collect these mushrooms, but I do think that in general the British don't know and probably are not bothered about knowing more about the different types of mushrooms.

When living in Devon, I remember doing my exercises one morning to a local radio station music programme. You know the type of morning music programme - when they ask you questions and invite you to phone in with the answer? I was obliviously working out in movement when all of a sudden there was a question about mushrooms and although I had never done anything like this before, I couldn't resist the temptation. I called, answered the question and was sent a prize – two latest chart discs!

Still thinking mushrooms, when I first came to Château Monplaisir, I felt quite apprehensive cooking for David. By this time I had been connected with France for such a long time that I live the French way of life.

I soon found out that David wasn't a lover of *cèpes*...... In fact, he didn't particularly like them – and that was that! I asked him why and he told me it was because of the texture which applied to the whole mushroom family. Well, we had to do something about this dilemma, so one night I grilled steak and in a frying pan I added some butter and olive oil – getting it very hot. I then added the *cèpes*. As soon as they were ready I sprinkled shredded parsley and garlic over them. Oh... said David, these mushrooms are very tasty....... Need I say more?

David later told me that we had *cèpes* in our woodlands and he let an elderly chap come to pick them. I suggested that we ought to ask this chap to give me some so I could store them in the freezer for that special dish.......

Later I discovered that our winemaker was filling old wine cartons full of them and I suppose he was giving them to all his friends. I was furious, "Charity begins at home" I informed David and asked him to arrange that a carton came up to the Château! One did, the next morning and I made a remark like "Thank you, I shall prepare these for the freezer". The winemaker was quite stunned finding out that I was 'into *cepes*' and more arrived the next day..... I am now considering a larger freezer! Perhaps he thought all the Brits were not *cèpes* fans.

Trompette des Morts

The second mushroom is *Trompette des Morts*. At first, I thought it was referring to death and wondered about the connection. It was later that I learned it was actually *Trompette des Morts* and the connection was that when the Moors invaded France they were carrying a trumpet which was used to signal death to the French and the trumpet was in the same shape as the mushroom, small, thin, flaring out at the end, dark in colour.

These mushrooms are delicious with a terrific flavour and in fact they can be used in dishes instead of *cèpes*, this is why they are sometimes referred to as the 'poor man's *cèpes*.'

One of my favourite dishes with this type of mushroom is an omelette with the chopped mushrooms added - and of course, a glass or two of good full bodied Bergerac Rouge.

Pied de la Mouton

The next mushroom I must write about is the *Pied de la Mouton*, a very delicate mushroom found at the base of certain trees.

The people next door to my farmhouse are from Marseilles and visit only a few times a year. They had a couple of trees cut down and in that particular autumn I noticed one or two locals making regular visits to the garden and collecting…..

When the gardener next called, I enquired about these visits and he told me that the trunk of one of the trees was covered in *Pied de la Mouton* every day. He continued to tell me how good these mushrooms are and I ought to collect them and prepare them for the freezer. Well - what an invitation! The first lot I picked I couldn't resist putting them into hot butter, frying them – then covering a toasted slice of fresh French bread with the results, thinking to myself – this is sheer extravagance!

After this, there was no stopping me – these delicious mushrooms went into fish dishes and all sorts of chicken delights.

La Morille

La Morille is yet another delight of the mushroom family and delectable in any meat dish served with red wine. I like to pick this mushroom off the plate – with a fork, of course, put it in my mouth and savour the flavour. It's on its own……..

Chapter: 9

My Special Dordogne Recipes

Garlic Soup

    2 tablespoons of goose fat
    12 fresh garlic cloves
    1½ litres [around 2 1/2 pints] chicken stock
    Bouquet garni
    Salt and freshly ground pepper
    3 eggs
    4 oz [near 100grams] Emmental cheese
    4 slices of toast

Melt fat, add garlic and sweat until light gold in colour. Don't burn.
Gradually pour in stock bouquet garni salt and pepper.
Simmer for 30 mins.

Remove, cool and liquidise.

Separate the eggs. Beat white, slowly add to soup.

Put egg yolks in bowl, slowly add two ladles of soup, mix and add to the soup.

Decorate with toast and cheese.

Chestnut Soup

1lb [half a kilo] of chestnuts or equivalent in
   canned chestnuts
I tablespoonful of goose fat
1 medium sized onion, chopped
1 celery stick, chopped
1 large garlic clove, chopped
1 litre [1 3/4 pints] of chicken stock
½ litre [under 1 pint] of milk
Salt and freshly ground pepper
4 tablespoons of fresh cream

Heat goose fat and gently fry onions, celery and garlic then add chestnuts, stock, milk and butter simmer for 45 mins. Liquidise. That's it!

Salad of Dandelion Leaves and Bacon

Young dandelion leaves [before flowering]
Salt and pepper
Lardons
Little vinaigrette

The secret is to pick the dandelion leaves at the right time and that is before the flowers appear. Young leaves are what you want.

Wash them and sprinkle with a little salt, pepper and chopped garlic.

In a frying pan, throw in a pack of prepared lardons [tiny sliced pieces of pork]. Fry until nice and crispy and then throw over the salad leaves – delicious!

Beetroot Salad

1 Pack of beetroot
1-2 Granny Smith apples [depending on size]
Olive oil
Cider vinegar
Garlic
Salt and pepper

This is what I call my healthy eating salad. I mix some olive oil, cider vinegar, salt, pepper and crushed garlic in a bowl.

I then chop up a couple of beetroot, a Granny Smith apple and mix together and pour over the olive oil mixture and put it in the fridge so that you can serve it truly cold.

Pommes Sarladais

Potatoes
Goose fat
Garlic [crushed and mixed with chopped parsley]
salt and pepper.

Fry the potatoes in the goose fat – this gives them that special flavour and when they are just about cooked add the other ingredients and serve.

Now my way is slightly different in so much as I cook some lardons in the goose fat with the potatoes – just adds a little more flavour.

Magret de Canard

Magret de Canard [I allow one for two persons]
Garlic and parsley
Salt and pepper

This is one of my favourite cuts of the duck. It is the breast, a thin layer of meat covered by a thick layer of fat.

For me, the best way to cook it is on a barbeque. You really need a high heat and to do this indoors means a messy, smelly kitchen unless you are one of the fortunate with all the special gadgets necessary to do the type of cooking.

I score the skin of the breast after seasoning it and cook on that side until a lot of the fat has disappeared – then I turn it over and just lightly grill the other side and pop it into a warm oven for a few minutes.

I like the meat just underdone, although my husband prefers it well done.

I watched Nigella Lawson preparing Magret de Canard during one of her television courses and was quite surprised to see that she stripped the meat from the fat before cooking. She actually cooked the meat in the duck fat – but this perhaps is the answer to cooking a Magret de Canard in the normal kitchen.

Confit de Canard

The pieces of Confit should be put on a tray and popped into a hot oven for as long as required to brown the skin. Care should be taken that they are not overdone – bearing in mind that the meat is already cooked and all you are doing is heating and crisping the skin.

This dish is the pride of the Dordogne……. Again going back in time, the villagers were well equipped for the duck season. Some still continue to prepare the duck but most have little time to spare. Times have changed and at the right time the supermarkets in Bergerac are full of local produce.

The first thing I must clarify is the horrible stories one hears about force feeding ducks and I know I am going to be blasted by many of you about this but ducks enjoy their life style… In fact, on many farms now they have a duck's self service restaurant!

The feeding pipes are fitted to the wall and when the ducks feel a pang of hunger, they come in and help themselves.

People who conserve duck have a strict procedure. In November, the duck farms are visited by the conservers. This is inspection time, as they want to check the quality of the duck and its size. This is when the orders are made.

It is not often you have a chance to taste Confit du Canard outside of France in the way that it is prepared in the Southwest. The pieces of duck with seasoning are put in kiln jars. The kiln jars are then put in boilers to cook the duck and sterilize it.

The ducks are then collected and taken home to where a special kitchen has been prepared to do this type of work. From one duck you will have magret du canard, confit du canard, foie gras, rillettes, paté and even a quantity of duck fat to use for cooking potatoes, etc. The French tell us that duck fat is good for you – much better than any other type of fat or oil we may use for cooking. It is not nearly as fattening – so they say… but I don't know…..!

Salade de Gésiers

When preparing a Dordogne lunch for British visitors my biggest problem is trying to serve an entrée such as Salade de Gésiers.

Most of the British will just not accept it – and the French think it is an absolute gastronomic delight if it is included in the menu. You can't win!

I think there are two reasons why it is not accepted. The first is that it is duck – and the majority of the British do not agree with the feeding methods of the animal. The second is the part of the body from which the gésiers come – the neck - and this French delicacy is not appreciated.

Actually I find a true salade des gésiers quite tasty – but I wouldn't want it every week – once in a while is acceptable.

Pot au Feu

The dish with most vegetables used is the Pot au Feu. This is
when you put a piece of inexpensive meat into a large pot and
add all the vegetables you can – not forgetting the garlic…. Let it
cook very slowly then serve the vegetables as a plate before the
main course – a great favourite in the winter. Sometimes, as you
do with the remains of vegetable soup, you add a little red wine
to the dish and sup it. In France we call this 'Faites le Chabrol'.

Clafouti

Fruit of choice
Butter
Flour
Eggs Sugar Milk

I do not get excited about this dish but it is a great way to use up
the cherries and plums as at certain times of the year we have
buckets full of them!

The first thing you have to do is prepare the fruit, ie, in the
case of the cherries, remove the stalks and wash – leave in the
stones….very important, I am told. With the plums – give them
a wash and stone them.

Then get a flat earthenware pie dish, butter it and sprinkle a
little flour into it – making sure that the base is covered.

Melt about 3oz [85gm] of butter in a pan and leave it to cool;
add what is left of the 4oz [115gm] of flour, four eggs and 3oz
[85gm]of sugar in a bowl add the melted butter and mix well.
Gradually warm 8 fl oz [230ml] of milk and add this to the rest
of the ingredients, mix well until it looks like a pancake mixture.
Leave the mixture for a couple of hours to settle and then arrange

the fruit in the dish and pour the mixture over. Bake in the oven 375/195/ Gas 5 for 40-45 minutes. When the Clafouti has cooled down, sprinkle it with icing sugar and serve.

Strawberries in Wine

This is a great favourite in season. All you have to do is prepare the fruit as normal – put them in a bowl and cover with caster sugar. Twenty minutes before serving, add your favourite sweet wine, Monbazillac or Saussignac, and put back in the fridge until ready to serve!

Prunes as a 'Digestif'

After every harvest of the plums, we are allowed to distil the prune juice to produce a l'eau de vie. This is strictly controlled and must be 'declared'. I would describe this l'eau de vie as perfumed fire water but I am told by my neighbours that this is a very good digestif to take after dinner. The male members of the family usually add it to the warm cup which the coffee has been served in and you would be surprised at the difference this makes to the firewater. Ladies usually dip a cube of sugar into the liquid – completely convinced of its powers to the digestive system!

I make use of the firewater in another way which also helps to use the plums we have in abundance.

I wash and dry the prunes and pack them into a jar – as big as I can find then cover the fruit with the said liquid.

I store the jars sealed for a couple of years – or even longer.

These are served just like the l'eau de vie in the warm coffee cup after dinner. One prune is quite enough although I have known guests to have many more!

Recently, a colleague of mine – another educator – brought a group of 29 to Bergerac to study wine. It was agreed that they would lunch on one of the days at Château Monplaisir. They arrived about one o'clock and sat down to lunch after chatting about the property and the work we do here. Lunch took several hours! At five o'clock I handed out coffee and asked if anyone would like to try a prune......... I unsealed the tall spaghetti jar and offered it around. There were very few left when the jar was returned – just as well that they came by coach!

Chapter 10

The Wines of Bergerac

Before we leave the subject of food in the south-west of France, I'd like to make a mention of when I recently dined in Paris in the restaurant of Hélène Darroze. A wonderful experience! After studying the menu I came to the conclusion that she is

the 'modern Michel Guérard' from the south-west of France, a chef I admired for many years. In fact, I have two of his books, *Gourmet Gourmand* and *Gourmet Minceur*.

My companions had great difficulty selecting their dishes as there was a full array of all the most delightful gastronomic plates of the south-west region and, because they had come from the UK, they did not have the opportunity as I have had of tasting all these specialities such as *foie gras, confit, magret* and more but I must say the presentation of each dish certainly took my interest.

During this year's hunting season, our winemaker, a keen *chasseur*, brought us a huge piece of venison from one particular hunt – this is common practice when someone shoots on your land. I took the piece of meat graciously and put it in the freezer, thinking to myself, how was I going to prepare it?

On Hélène's menu that evening in Paris, there was a *chevreuil* and I decided to select this dish so that I could obtain some idea of how the meat should taste when cooked to perfection – and this was! My plate arrived with three pieces of meat, one was a small cut of rib and the other two were like fillet. The *chevreuil* was accompanied with a wine sauce and vegetables in season. I have never tasted such tender meat and the rich flavours stayed in my mouth until the next morning – even after cleaning my

teeth on return to the hotel!

To my surprise, when handed the wine list, I found several Bergerac wines – vineyards well known to me and this pleased me very much. The price of these wines were in the highest bracket I have ever seen, but they were in comparison with the rest of the wines on the list and I felt that at last I had seen respect given to the quality wines of Bergerac.

This is the first time I have dined outside the south-west and still thought I was in the south-west – if this makes sense to you. It was a delightful evening, one I shall remember and a restaurant to which I plan to return.

To find Hélène's restaurant, take the metro to Sèvres-Babylone, or email to darroze@relaischateaux.fr.

People are at last finding out about Bergerac wines!

Added to finding a good selection of Bergerac wines in the restaurant in Paris, I was thrilled to read about our wines in the OLN [Off-Licence Newspaper]. I am fortunate enough to receive a copy of the OLN every month – it keeps me up to date with the trade.

Just lately, they issued a very good little booklet entitled *Choose France – The retailer's essential guide to the world of French wine*. I enjoyed reading about the wines in the south-west – especially those from in and around Bergerac where it states:

> 'In Bergerac in the Dordogne, wines are made in a number of styles which bear a close resemblance to those of nearby Bordeaux. The reds, such as Pécharmant, Montravel Rouge and Côtes de Bergerac – made from Cabernet Sauvignon, and Cabernet Franc, along with some Merlot and Malbec – could be mistaken for those of some of Bordeaux's satellite appellations. The dry wines deserve attention, ranging from relatively light, crisp quaffers to weighty, rich ripe wines that command immense respect among the cognoscenti. Bergerac appellations such as Monbazillac and Saussignac make sweet white wines that can stand up to those of Sauternes in sweet richness – although never the same price.'

How about that? Three cheers for OLN.

When I first came to live in France, I was still making my own wine. Getting the *must* to the right temperature was no problem in the warmer climate; the fermentation started and kept going, with a little stir each day.

My neighbours watched on in amazement. The incredible British! They were mesmerised by the hanging marrow, the potatoes rotting happily and the airlocks on the demijohns. Well, that called for a photograph or two!

It was a morning, during the *vendange*, when I opened the back door and found a large rubbish bin full of grapes that I realised they were not so much amazed by my adroitness, but sympathetic as I had no vines in my garden! Needless to say that was the end of my winemaking – but in hindsight, it may have been the time when I should have bought a few hectares!

I gave up making wine not long after I came to live in the Dordogne. My neighbours thought it very amusing to find wine being made with rice, tea, carrots etc., but when a rather wise paysant friend came to visit he told me that I must stop immediately because it is against the law to ferment wine without permission. So, after finishing the potato liqueur, I hung up my demijohns and fermentation locks and never used them again. The winemaking episode of my life had finished. That is until recently.

When I married David and started to become involved in the winemaking at Monplaisir, I had to be very careful as our winemaker is one of the typical French we describe as 'male chauvinist'. My knowledge and experience of wine seemed to worry him at first but now he has accepted this. Fortunately, David and I work together in the business: I advise and he administers. Quite a good arrangement!

David had very little knowledge about wine when he first came to Monplaisir – in fact he had none! As time has gone on, I have surreptitiously educated him – not to certificate level but enough for him to know what those around are talking about. Included in his education have been several visits to vineyards in other regions of France, and the New World.

We had just returned from the Côtes du Rhône in 2003 when our winemaker reported that the red wine from the 2002 harvest was looking very promising. At that time our barrels, which we had bought from Château Haut Brion after one year of use, were now four years old and getting near to 'garden furniture'!

Recently, our winemaker had been to an exhibition where he met up with a professional 'barrel scraper' who convinced him that if he scraped our barrels we could get more use out of them. I wasn't convinced, but he was given permission to proceed with the scraping of thirty barrels. There was obviously some tannin left in the wood, because Haut Brion uses only the best oak and even after four years there was something left.

In our recent trip, we had visited a winery where the wine

had been left in oak for eighteen months, which quite impressed me. Putting wine into new barrels for eighteen months could be a disaster but I started thinking about our older barrels and the promising wine of 2002.

I suggested to David that we did just that. Put the wine into barrels for eighteen months as a trial. Our winemaker wasn't happy about this as it meant that we couldn't age the following year's wine in oak. I didn't think the barrels would age another year's wine! So David and I went ahead with our plan. It was quite exciting!

At the end of the period, a sample of wine was brought in for us to taste. Oh dear! Raw was putting it mildly. But my experience told me that this might work. The wine was bottled.

The following year, a colleague of mine came down from London and I told her about this very special wine. Immediately she said, "We must open a bottle." We brought one from the *chai* [winery] and opened it well in advance and decanted it – nice and high so that the air could get through.

During dinner we tasted it and all my fears had gone, this was a very good bottle of wine – agreed by all. I decided to name the wine 'Cuvée Hélène'. The remaining tannin in the oak was just enough to age the wine and by doing it slowly gave roundness and softness as well as an intense depth of colour that we have not had with any of our wines before. This was certainly a 'one-off', the barrels used for this wine are now tables, seats and flower buckets in the garden.

As stated in my first book, *Winewoman @ Bergerac.France*, I have been flying the flag for this area for so many years and backing Bergerac wines.

Bergerac benefited tremendously when in 1255, Henry III, the King of England, included Bergerac in his jurisdiction. This privilege gave the right to free travel for all in the region. The Bordelaise were not very happy with this and objected strongly – especially about the free movement of wine. Bergerac was in a very interesting position because it was able to send its wines to England and Holland but refused to accept any other wines into Bergerac!

The region suffered very much from the Revolution, phylloxera and more recently in 1956 from a freeze-up which took the temperature down to between minus 27° and 30°. This cold period lasted for over three weeks and there was a metre deep of snow which halted the movement of goods into the region. The vines couldn't take such low temperatures and the result was devastation in the vineyards.

In the 1970s Bergerac was a poor market town but wine has always been produced here since the Middle Ages. Bergerac is the wine-growing capital of the Dordogne, and there are around ninety-three villages with approximately 1,300 hectares under vine. Before the seventies a great deal of this land was under cattle, if this makes sense. Just as they did in Canada with the fruit farms when they realised that making wine was more profitable.

I know some wines to be of poor quality but am also aware of the quality wines which have been available for a long time but until recently were unknown to the British.

The reason for this is simple; the price was not attractive to négociants who were selling on the UK market. They wanted good profit and, because there is an imaginary ceiling price on the wines of Bergerac in supermarkets and some retail outlets, this can only be done with the cheaper-priced wines which are usually poorer in quality. The 'top of the range' wines of Bergerac are much higher quality. Unfortunately, the quality wines are lesser known. There are a few in restaurants and reputable wine stores but, because of poor publicity, UK wine drinkers are unaware of the range of wines which can be found in Bergerac.

I have been talking about these wines in the UK for 'yonks' years at different venues all over the country, always having to convince wine enthusiasts that the wines presented were actually from Bergerac. At these talks, or wine presentations, there has always been great discussion about the difference in the quality of the wines which I had brought for tasting and those found in the supermarkets. I wasn't at all surprised!

Knowing the workings of the British market in the past, the general idea was to fill the shelves with a lesser quality wine at a low price to encourage people to buy – good marketing, especially with the young wine buyers. But, the down point of this was that the buyers accepted this as a Bergerac wine and the reputation of the wines of Bergerac was pretty low.

I got sick of writing to wine traders and others who described the wines as 'country wines'. Was it impossible for people to understand that Bergerac wines are AOC (Appellation d'Origine Contrôlée)? But this reputation continued, and the majority of Bergerac wines in the supermarket were of lesser quality and not the type which you would buy a second time. This was a major contribution towards harming the reputation. One poor wine can put you off completely. Restaurants or hotels, where more individual expertise is used in selecting wines, are where you find the quality wines of Bergerac.

It was such people as Henry Ryman, Luc de Conti, François-Xavier de Saint-Exupéry, Laurence de Bosredon and, later, Richard Doughty and Charles Martin, who managed to penetrate the British market so that it was accepted by the UK wine trade that Bergerac had quality wines. So, if truth be known, it wasn't done by publicity, it was 'hard slog' by the aforementioned and the 'proof' is now for all to see.

I suppose the first daylight came with Henry Ryman some twenty years ago, but recently there has been a huge upsurge and I think that the main reason is the type of winemaker we now have, and the conception of cheap flights into Bergerac. We no longer have to depend on inadequate advertising. The reason I give no credit to the publicity of Bergerac wines is because it has been so poor right from the start.

One of my biggest shocks regarding 'Bergerac Wine Publicity' was on passing through the Metro in Paris, as I often did when working with wine groups. On this particular occasion the walls of the Metro were covered with advertising for the wines of Bergerac. This is amazing, I thought to myself; it must have cost a fortune and is it the right place to advertise?

When I write or talk about CIVRB, some are of the opinion that I am continually criticising them and I suppose I am to a certain extent. But what CIVRB must realise is that I am looking at it from the other side and all I want to do is help to improve the generally poor reputation of the wines of Bergerac. They have been part of my life for thirty years and I have truly supported

the work of the producers.

To me, their biggest problem has been lack of experienced staff in administration. There seem to be far too many changeovers of staff and most in the hub, apart from one or two, are very young with very little knowledge of wine outside Bergerac. This is not just recently, it has been going on for years.

Good publicists are expensive but necessary, just look at Piat d'Or. The marketing of that must have cost a fortune, but they have made a fortune from the wine sales. And don't ask me what I think of the wine!

I would like to see more of the vignerons' money being directed into publicity, especially now when more Bergerac wine is going into the UK market. I was speaking to one of our top wine producers who considers that the money for publicity was not enough and sometimes wasted. For example, invitations sent out to celebrities who have very little to do with wine and are not likely to help with marketing it.

A suggestion that this money would be better spent in sending representatives, that is Bergerac wine producers, to wine shows in, say, Germany, Spain or Italy to promote the wines of Bergerac, is one very good idea, but there are several others. And I would like to add that more Bergerac producers be helped to attend these events.

During the many years, at different venues all over the UK, much of the time was spent convincing wine enthusiasts that the wines I was presenting were actually from Bergerac and not from Bordeaux or even Jersey, as quite a few who spent some time in front of the 'telly' thought!

I am pleased to say that there is now a new generation of winemakers in Bergerac. Much to my pleasure I keep hearing of visits to New World wine regions by these winemakers. They know the importance of 'being involved' with what is going on in the world – competing and selling their wines in these and other countries. What has even made it more interesting is that winemakers from the New World are buying vineyards in Bergerac!

At last we seem to be getting out of 'living in the shadows of Bordeaux', as has been the general opinion of most in Bergerac but, as long as there are vignerons in Bergerac who are permitted to make an inferior wine and sell it for poor prices, this is going to take time. Those buying the inferior wine will look upon Bergerac wine as a cheap wine and the reputation will rest there. Do these producers of low grade wines know what they are doing?

You would be truly surprised if you knew the prices offered by négociants from Holland, Belgium, Germany and France, even with quality wines. I have only one word to describe these prices: insulting!

There is no consideration or respect given for the price of producing the wine, the bottle, label, cork, capsule and the contents.

I shall give you an example. You may sell a wine at your chateau for, say, a Bergerac Sec, €5 or 6 a bottle. A négociant will buy it from you to put in the supermarket with a selling price of €3. He will probably offer you €1 per bottle [if you are lucky] and the négociant isn't bothered; if he doesn't get the wine from one vigneron he'll soon get it from elsewhere. Ditto the supermarket.

I don't think the négociant makes a lot of profit as the supermarkets have very keen prices, but when you're talking of hundreds of bottles, in some cases thousands, someone is making a decent profit and it is not the producer, who is hardly getting enough to cover the cost of producing it!

But isn't this an agricultural pattern? You may also be interested to know that in some cases the négociant is responsible for filling the shelves with the wine he has sold to the supermarket! To add to this, it is not the supermarket's staff who man the wine fetes held in the store – the négociants involved in the wine stock have a rota for each day of the wine fair or promotion.

However, going back to the quality wines of Bergerac, I should like to give you an example of how good the quality is and yet unknown to even our neighbours.

The WSET® [Wine and Spirit Education Trust] has become international and has now expanded into France. There is a school in Burgundy and the one at Château Monplaisir is the Centre in south-west France. I had my first French student only recently, a young girl, eager to study wine marketing in one of the very good colleges in the UK. When she applied she was advised to take the WSET Intermediate Certificate. She found out about me on the Internet and phoned to ask if it was possible; I said yes and she came to Monplaisir to study.

During the time of study, she tasted our 1998 Côtes de Bergerac Rouge, liked it very much and bought a few bottles. A few days later she arrived to tell me that she had arranged a wine tasting in Bordeaux the evening before with some of her colleagues and, to her amazement, not one of her colleagues thought the 1998 was a wine from Bergerac. A much superior wine, they thought, than – dare I say it – Bergerac.

We depend on CIVRB to look after the control in our vineyards and vinification, up to the point of achieving our AOC. In this arrangement we pay not only an annual fee but also a fee for each time they provide advice and analyse our wines. We have had several problems with the oenologists appointed to Château Monplaisir. In the eight years we have been in Bergerac we have had five oenologists and all but one has come to us straight from college.

One was made redundant because he was considered too young by the customers, yet he produced our 1997 oaked red discussed earlier. Another oenologist retired due to pressure from the vignerons in a difficult year. A later one had to be rejected by us and then, after this, a young female oenologist moved to Bordeaux – smart lady. I would like to think this was due to the chat I had with her when she first joined us, but it wasn't – her boyfriend from Bordeaux persuaded her.

On one occasion, we complained bitterly about the competence of the appointed oenologist and, to our shock, immediately a change was made to a more senior member of staff, but after about four weeks we were informed that his assistant was appointed to look after us. She had just finished her wine education and was completely without experience!

I find this most unacceptable. We have a choice: we either support the CIVRB or employ an outside oenologist.

To give you an example of what inexperience can lead to, one young oenologist told us that the Moelleux we had produced for that particular year was poor and we ought to ditch it by sending it to the distillery. We were not happy about this decision and our winemaker decided to filter it. The wine got its AOC Saussignac first time and two years later received a gold medal award!

I am of the opinion that CIVRB should apply the same type of ruling to their oenologists as they do to the vines, that is the juice of young vines is not allowed to be vinified until the vine is five years of age, and that's how I feel about an oenologist; they shouldn't be allowed out on their own until they have had five years' apprenticeship with a senior member of staff.

I can assure you that there are major changes ahead for the wines of Bergerac and the arrow is pointing upwards. There are many more quality wine producers than we have ever had before and even the wine region itself is taking on an air of grace. Some of the wine chateaux which have been neglected in the past have been and are now being renovated. I also feel that the dividing line between quality wine producers and the lesser is now becoming wider.

The producers of the wines of Bergerac are having problems like all the other regions of France. French wines are certainly underpriced in France but overpriced outside France – which tells us something.

A few weeks ago, I wrote to one of the officials in Bergerac, asking if I could visit him to discuss the problems. I didn't receive a reply. But just recently, there have been *manifestations* [marches] in Bergerac concerning the marketing of wines. For instance, the producers are against wines being sold for €1 per bottle and feel there should be some type of legislation to determine a minimum price that the wines of Bergerac should be sold for in the supermarket. I agree entirely, but look what they're up against.

Just recently, a promotion flyer from one of the supermarkets was put in our post box. It was offering: 'For every six bottles of Bordeaux wine bought at 34 euros, you would get another twelve free!'

You may ask me how they are able to do this. Here is a possible answer.

In France, if you have produced too much wine, or you have wine that you cannot sell, there are companies willing to take this wine from you but it must be labelled, capsuled and in cartons. They will then buy it from you at a disgusting price, like €0.50–0.80 a bottle and, more often than not, you have to pay for the transport to the depot. This could well be one of the suppliers of very cheap wine to the supermarkets.

I'm sure that vignerons selling their wine at these ridiculously low prices have no idea of the damage they are creating. However, they probably need the money and have problems stocking old wines when new lines become available. Thank goodness they are in the minority. But to give you yet another example, digest the following:

In 2003 a supermarket in Bergerac advertised in their customer catalogue, which is sent out regularly, that there was a special offer of Bergerac AOC wine at €1 per bottle. That is around 60p and this doesn't cover the cost of the bottle, label, cork and capsule – never mind the wine.

"This is too much," were the words the President of the CIVRB uttered at a recent Assembly. "The supermarket catalogue advertised a Bergerac AOC wine for €1 a bottle!"

What price did the supermarket actually pay for it? I have no idea but the production could not have been covered. Anyway, this was considered as a real insult to the wines of Bergerac and the President of the Federation said that this national publicity was scandalous.

So, what was the outcome?

A group of viticulturists went to the stores in question, collected a trolley each, then proceeded to the wine shelves and removed every bottle of this underpriced wine. By the time the trolleys went through the cash desks there wasn't a bottle left!

One would automatically think that there was very little profit in it but consider the thousands and thousands of bottles. Then, of course, you have to consider the vigneron who has produced too much wine. He has to store it and if it doesn't sell he is left with valuable storage space he is unable to use for his new wine. He must get rid of the older wine and turns to the négociants who are willing to buy it.

What is the Answer?

As far as I am concerned, and you may think I am self-opinionated, a change is really necessary. Bergerac has created a poor image of itself by selling its wines at a ridiculously low price and not showing more of its quality wines.

There are several ways of doing something about this but, no matter which way it is done, many producers will suffer from the changes. In the long run, it will be a good thing. There are too many vineyards in Bergerac and, what with the political and worldwide regard, something must be done for the whole of the French wine industry.

Fédération of Vignerons Indépendants

We are also members of the Fédération des Vignerons Indépendants [FVI] of Dordogne who have their offices on the east side of Bordeaux. We have found them most helpful when assistance has been needed.

For example, we were caught up with the thirty-five-hour week problem which reigned in France for a few years. We had a team of three workers and one insisted on working the thirty-five-hour week. He is the type who offers no flexibility in his working hours.

We agreed that he should work nine days every two weeks thus having one Monday off per two weeks. This worked very well with a team of three; there were always two on duty. Unfortunately, the team of three became a team of two when one was forced into early retirement because of illness. This meant that every second Monday there was only one on duty and this led to difficulties when most jobs required two workers. Why did you not hire a third as a replacement might be asked? The third worker was often absent due to illness – bad back, etc. In fact, it was because of one of his long absences when we thought he wouldn't return that we were forced to take on another worker. This meant we had an extra worker [one more than required for the number of hectares we have]. It wasn't long before he applied for early retirement due to illness and left. This left us in an awkward situation because every second Monday we had only one worker instead of two –which led to difficulties when heavy machinery had to be moved. We couldn't have the other worker on a 35 hour week when we only had two workers.

The situation went on for months, in fact, a couple of years and, although it was obvious we were having problems, our thirty-five-hour worker made no offer to resolve the situation by coming back to work every second Monday.

Then things became desperate; the thirty-nine-hour worker said he must have help every day. We didn't want to cause any ill feeling but this law, giving the option of working thirty-five hours, wasn't clear, so we contacted the FVI and asked for advice.

It came within days and with other help included in order to help us approach the worker which resulted in an immediate return to thirty-nine hours.

David doesn't attend many of the FVI meetings simply because of language difficulties. Now I'm not saying that our French is poor, because it is not, but when you get a load of country people together speaking in *patois* – that is difficult.

Anyway, we decided to make the effort recently. The AGM invitation asked us to be at the venue for 9.15 a.m. but, knowing the French, we arrived at 9.25 a.m. to find that very few members had turned up but were trickling in, and this went on until just before 10 a.m. when the meeting started.

It was the usual procedure: minutes of the last meeting to be approved, then on to the business of the day. They couldn't get the portable computer to work so we sat looking at a blank overhead projector screen until the technician got it working.

The meeting was in progress and the main discussion at that point was on the recent drastic fall in sales and export of wines. They couldn't understand why Champagne is doing so well on the market, having to produce more and the other regions are suffering.

The next item was about updating the publicity to attract more members to the Federation. They felt that the publicity must be more approachable than before. The new leaflets looked quite attractive but I wasn't convinced that this was the way to bring in new members.

The next item was help to those wishing to enter the market with details of courses offered by the Federation to assist those who wanted to be able to find the markets, contact people, etc. There were different costs for each course, I found these quite expensive and felt that perhaps the Government ought to subsidise them.

Time was speeding by and there had been no break for coffee or a comfort visit. We had been sitting in the same chair for three hours! Then to my surprise, one of the representatives of a large insurance company in Bergerac was allowed to try and sell his wares and we were subjected to projected tables of savings, etc. As he continued to tell the vignerons how they covered all aspects of loss, one member who had obviously been 'done' by insurance tried to get the rep to define the losses covered in a vineyard, that is, related to AOC and non-AOC vineyards. I couldn't get the whole story because people started shouting and arguing.

It ended up being quite embarrassing for the representative and the chairman cleverly brought the discussion to a close by introducing the *Préfet* of the Dordogne, M Bartolt, to say the final few words. We had actually been sitting for nearly four hours before the meeting ended.

Robert Parker has even reached Bergerac – he once wrote that he thought that Saussignac sweet wines were one of France's 'hidden secrets'. Vignerons voice different opinions of him but I agree with him that French winemakers mustn't dwell on their history, they must use that history, tradition, call it what you like, as a basis for coming into the modern world.

France produces some of the best wines in the world but the producers must face reality in that it is a cut-throat world out there and you must compete. Many French wine drinkers have never tasted wines from outside their country. I can understand this to a certain degree, for reasons of protection and loyalty, but this is no good for the wine producer who wants to target the world market – he's got to know the force he is competing with and the people of France should also have more idea of what is going on in the real world.

If French supermarkets offered a better selection of 'other' wines so that consumers could taste what their producers were challenging, then a better understanding of what the long-suffering French wine producers are dealing with would probably result in a major rethink on all fronts.

Well, that is my opinion and I know that many will not agree with it but when I see how much work is being done by these enthusiastic 'new generation' Bergerac vignerons, I feel more recognition and help should be given to push them forward.

Chapter 11

Climate of Bergerac

The climate of Bergerac is similar to that of the south-west of England, but a few degrees warmer.

December, January and February are usually miserable with rain, heavy mists and possibly very cold periods. Visitors are amazed when told that temperatures can be as low as minus 10° and, on occasions, even lower. I have experienced minus 20°. From February, it starts to improve so there is a chance of plenty of sunshine and very pleasant days thereafter. I must add that there can also be a lot of rain during this period – it is often raining at Easter. The French country people tell me that Easter is the week of sadness and this is why it rains or is a very windy period.

As June peeps its head up we get evidence of summer being on its way. Then we have glorious, warm weather, even hot to very hot, right into September. This warm weather can spread on into October and November: shorts and T-shirt are not uncommon wear, even at the beginning of November.

The Dordogne is notorious for storms – freak storms and tornadoes are not uncommon. In fact, over the years, I have seen many. French insurance companies suffer more claims in this region than in any other part of France. At one time, modems, fax machines, kitchen electrical equipment were replaced nearly

every year because of thunder and lightning attacks. This has forced the EDF [the electricity board] to put overhead cables underground where possible.

Hailstorms are also regular occurrences and, of course, these can be devastating for the vines at the wrong time of the season. The hailstones are often the size of golf balls and are capable of wiping out vineyards in minutes. The vignerons fear these storms most of all in the month of July when such devastation can be at its most severe.

There are the occasional dry years, such as 2003 and 2005. There was no rain from May until September in 2005. The vines could cope with this but the plum orchards, cornfields and others suffered terribly.

In general, August and September are calm months with good weather. You can get odd periods of rain but this is usually spasmodic. This is why it is best to own your own grape harvester which unfortunately not many people can afford. With one of these machines at your disposal, you can pick at the right time, that is, in brief, when warm for red grapes and early morning, when it is cool, for the white grapes but never in the rain as this dilutes the wine. If you have to rely on hiring a machine, this can lead to problems and the main one is rain during the hiring period.

October and November are the sad months for me. When the harvest is over, the white grape vine leaves turn to a yellowy gold and the red to a rich auburn colour – it looks magnificent in the sunshine. Regrettably, we are not able to enjoy this sight for very long because autumn is here and the winds strip the vines of all their glory in a very short time.

Soil of Bergerac

There are many different soils in this region and I am pleased to say that they are being well studied by the appropriate authorities. I heard recently that about forty vineyards have already had their soil analysed in order to improve their production. This was wonderful music to my ears, as Bergerac producers are now showing how serious they are at producing quality wines.

The soil in general in the Bergerac region is gravel, sand, alluvium deposits, calcareous, *argile* (clay) and ancient marine fossils being due to the, at one time, massive coverage of water in south-west France.

The right bank of the Dordogne, the Pécharmant region of Bergerac, is quite different from the left bank of the Dordogne. The soil is much deeper and is ferruginous – mixed with *argile*. It is sandier, and more *argile-calcaire* [chalk] with gravel in the high areas.

If you are in the region and are interested in the soil, you must visit Château Renaudie where the owner has an excellent collection of what he has found in the soil of his vineyards.

South of the River Dordogne is quite different as it is heavy

with clay, chalk and limestone, in fact, there are four different layers of *calcaire* [limestone]. These *calcaires* are described as, *calcaire de Monbazillac, calcaire d'Issigeac*, etc. If you study some of the old farmhouses in the region you will see evidence of this because these houses were built from the stones found in the ground.

In the 1970s Bergerac was a poor market town but wine has always been produced here since the Middle Ages. Bergerac is the wine-growing capital of the Dordogne, and there are around ninety-three villages with approximately 1,300 hectares under vine.

In the seventies the cattle farms started to transform and become vineyards. I witnessed a similar situation when I studied the vineyards of Niagara on the Lake in Canada where the fruit farms became vineyards over a period of time, the owners realising that making wine was more profitable.

Today, the Dordogne is responsible for only 2.6 per cent by land area and 2.4 per cent by volume of all AOC French wines. The average vineyard covers 12.4 hectares or 30 acres. Some 52 per cent of these vineyards are under 10 hectares which brings into question their viability when some 60 per cent of Bergerac wine is sold *en vrac* – or in bulk rather than bottles.

When farmers changed over from cattle to vines it meant clearing the ground before planting the vines. I saw a lot of this being done. Tractors with a type of digger attached would dig up huge quantities of limestone and a chalky stone which turns dark once it is exposed to the air. Some of the stones were enormous, like huge rocks, and were used to decorate the gardens. This can be seen as you drive through the vineyard villages.

The smaller ones, although still quite large, were piled high and used for building. Nowadays this type of stone is scarce and to face the outside of a new house in natural stone is a very costly business.

There is a lot of clay and limestone on the north facing hillsides which is good for the white grapes, but you will find limestone for the red on the southern flank of the hillside.

To explain it in more detail:

1) Red grapes are planted in clay and limestone – with certain areas of Merlot – clay and silica.

2) White grapes are planted in clay and *boulbènes* (a hard soil found in the Dordogne, Cognac and Armagnac areas). I am not sure and have no proof but, being present in the areas mentioned, I get the impression *boulbènes* may help with the acidic content of the grape juice.

3) Pécharmant: Argilo-calcaire and gravel in the high areas, sand content. This soil is ideal for the rich red Pecharmant wines produced in this area.

Chapter 12

The Appellations of Bergerac

Many people argue with me about the AOC and believe it should be scrapped. I don't agree with this; perhaps there are one or two things I would change but, as far as soil is concerned, I do believe that there are certain types of soil for each variety of grape for optimum production. The other point you have to consider is the climate.

To give you an example, the Pinot Noir grape [literally 'Black Pine' and so named because the shape of the bunch is similar to that of a pine cone] grows extremely well in cooler climates, such as Burgundy. It wouldn't produce as well in Bordeaux or Bergerac.

The governing body of the AOC controls which grapes are grown in each region and I think this is good thinking. For instance, in Burgundy only grapes such as Pinot Noir, Chardonnay and Aligoté can have AOC on the label. You can produce wine from other grapes but they will not have AOC status.

Now this happened in Bergerac when Henry Ryman, the father of Hugh, decided to produce wine from another *cépage* [variety], other than those under the AOC of Bergerac. Henry was told that the wine couldn't be labelled as AOC and therefore would have less chance of selling because wines without AOC are looked upon as inferior wines. As it so transpired, Henry's wines had become so popular in the UK the non-AOC wine had sold immediately after it was bottled.

There was a similar incident in Languedoc. Daumas Gassac non-AOC wines were selling for much higher prices than AOC wines.

AOC means that all wines made in France are controlled and this was introduced at the end of 1935 and beginning of 1936. Each area of Bergerac has an AOC but it was introduced at different times, as follows:

AOC Introduction

Bergerac		1936
Monbazillac		1936
Pécharmant		1946
Rosette		1946
Montravel		1948
Saussignac		1982

It should be noted that Bergerac had its own appellation, Grand Cru, up to the early 1930s before the AOC we know today was introduced in 1936. You can see such Grand Cru bottles of that period in Château Monbazillac. It is well worth noting that Château Corbiac was a Pécharmant Premier Cru at that time. As mentioned in another part of the book, many vignerons would like the Grand Cru restored. I believe there have been discussions but nothing has yet been decided.

At the moment, there are thirteen AOCs of Bergerac wine and six of these are direct Bergerac AOCs.

The direct Bergerac AOCs are as follows:

Bergerac Rosé

Bergerac Sec

Bergerac Rouge

Côtes de Bergerac Moelleux

Côtes de Bergerac Rouge

Monbazillac

Then, at Bergerac, on the right bank of the River Dordogne, there are:

Pécharmant

Rosette

On the slopes of the left side, just south-west of Bergerac, is the sweet wine area of

Saussignac

On the same side, but north of Ste Foy La Grande, you will find:

Côtes de Montravel

Haut Montravel

Montravel

Montravel Rouge

Bergerac Rouge and Côtes de Bergerac Rouge – 'to be or not to be'

I am often asked about Bergerac Rouge and Côtes de Bergerac Rouge: What is the difference? This to me is a very good question because it is not at all clear to the uninitiated.

The answer is that the quality of the Côtes de Bergerac is

higher than the Bergerac Rouge. The production is different in that from each hectare of vines, less wine is produced for Côtes de Bergerac (50 hl/ha) than for Bergerac Rouge (60 hl/ha), thus the Côtes de Bergerac is of better quality. The Côtes de Bergerac also has a higher minimum alcohol content (11°) than the Bergerac Rouge (10°).

I cannot understand why the Bergerac authorities don't permit a Grand Cru now, as they had in the thirties. It would certainly be much clearer to 'Joe Public' if the Côtes de Bergerac was named Grand Cru: he would know instantly that this is the top quality of Bergerac AOC.

Some in the hierarchy say that to use this term would be pretentious but that statement doesn't make sense. Côtes de Bergerac is the quality wine of Bergerac and is entitled to the Grand Cru status.

Pécharmant AOC

This area was declared AOC in 1946, ten years after the wines were introduced.

The wines are red, produced from the Merlot and Cabernet Sauvignon. They have a good structure and these strong oaky wines need time to develop. Several years of ageing will result in a round, complex wine with loads of character. The colour is the most intense you will find in Bergerac.

Pécharmant was the best red wine of Bergerac up until the mid-eighties. Some of it is still in this category, but this is now along with other wines of Bergerac, especially the Côtes de Bergerac which have improved during recent times and quite a few of the Côtes are superior to the Pécharmants.

This area produces a highly respected wine which will age well and shouldn't be drunk young. It is best to keep these wines for about five years before drinking. It is described as: 'Fleshy, with great aromatic intensity and perfect for beef, duck, game and strong cheese'.

Pécharmant [meaning 'charming hill'] is situated on the right bank of the Dordogne and is the oldest, indeed the first, wine region in Bergerac. The soil is much sandier and women are in control of one or two of the vineyards, similar to the 'Champagne Widows'. Two or three widows of Pécharmant producers were left to continue with the viticulture and vinification on their husbands' deaths. In those days the production was truly 'traditional' with everything giving tannin going into the vat. I remember François-Xavier de Saint-Exupéry of Château Tiregand explaining how he managed to introduce more modern methods into the vinification, but he insisted that his mother always has the final say in the blending of these superb wines.

The Pécharmant region of Bergerac is a region which would much prefer to be set aside from Bergerac because of the history attached to it, but I don't agree. Pécharmant was the best red wine of Bergerac for many years. Some of it is still in the category of the best wines of Bergerac, but others are not as during recent years there has been tremendous progress with the wines from this region and a few of the Côtes de Bergerac winemakers respect the fact that Pécharmant was the flagship for Bergerac at one time and have used the reputation as a benchmark in the progress of production for all Bergerac wines. Nowadays, some of the Côtes de Bergeracs are superior to the lesser Pécharmants and compare with the better ones.

Pécharmant is included in three wine areas of Bergerac on the right bank of the Dordogne where the soil is quite different. I suppose, to explain better, similar to that of St Emilion which is on the same side. There is more sand in the soil.

Bergerac Alcohol Control

Wine	Minimum Alcohol	Maximum Alcohol	Resid. Sugar	
Bergerac Sec	10°	13°	4 grams	
Bergerac Rouge	10°	13°	2 grams	
Côtes de Bergerac	11°	13°	4-17 grams	
Moelleux	12°	16°	17-35 grams	
Liquoreaux	12°	18°	>54 grams	

Wine Sales 2002 to 2005

Wines Sold	2002/3	2003/4	2004/5	
Bergerac Rouge	295, 184	281, 808	314, 168	
Bergerac Rosé	26, 915	35, 391	35, 077	
Montravel Rouge	104	450	425	
Pécharmant	15,342	15,513	11,943	
Bergerac Sec	105,765	96,393	94,021	
Montravel	8,868	7,970	7,639	
C de B Moelleux	71,604	66,129	74,512	
Haut Montravel	1,194	1,736	1,336	
Côtes de Montravel	874	1,164	1,024	
Rosette	319	493	499	
Saussignac	1,094	959	818	
Monbazillac	51,501	46,603	47,891	
Côtes de Bergerac	11,406	10,126	8,214	
Total	241,219	221,447	227,740	
Grand Total	590,170	564,735	597,567	

The wine of Bergerac in the seventies and eighties was poor and no way could you compare the quality with the heavy tannic wine of Pécharmant. But there again, no way could you drink the wine of Pécharmant until it was much older because of the rough tannins. Unfortunately by the time the tannins had softened, the fruit was on its way out!

Monbazillac AOC

The first thing you notice about a good Monbazillac is the colour; as gold as the sun and this colour is enhanced as it deepens with age. Monbazillac can reach 15° alcohol content quite easily and I've witnessed 18°. The bouquet is of honey and acacia and there is a fullness on the palate.

The versatility of these wines is amazing: superb as an aperitif, with a dessert and *obligatoire* with foie gras. It is also excellent with Roquefort cheese.

These wines are produced by leaving the grapes on the vines until they are rotten. We call it Noble Rot – or *pouriture noble* in French. This process leaves the grape skins to shrink and concentrates the juice. The grapes are then picked by hand when the weather is dry and pressed before fermentation begins. Fermentation is stopped before completion in order to leave residual sugar in the wine.

These wines can age for years. In fact, bottles of this wine are given for christening presents so that the child will be able to drink it on his marriage, coming of age, etc.

Monbazillac wines were at one time the sweet wines of Britain's royal family, as was Sauternes to the Russian court. In fact, if you look around Château Monbazillac you will see a photograph of the Queen Mother taken on a visit many years ago and the guide will tell you that, "It was when she came down to top up an order"!

Rosette AOC

This area is between La Force and Bergerac and produces rich, soft white wine with a flowery, fruity bouquet. The wine is slightly straw-like in colour. A very nice wine as an aperitif or accompaniment to a mushroom dish.

This has always been the lesser-known AOC of Bergerac.

Bergerac Sec AOC

These wines are best drunk young when they are fresh and aromatic. The exception is Bergerac Sec produced from older vines [shown on the bottle as vieilles vignes], these will age longer and in time can change character slightly to offer a mature type of dry wine.

Bergerac Rosé AOC

This is a wonderful summer-drinking wine, especially as an aperitif. It is also excellent with Chinese food.

I think my main love of these wines is the acidity level. It is not as harsh like so many other rosés and the delicate aroma of strawberries on the nose continues on to the palate.

It is best to drink it young and a good rosé will drink well even in the second year – if you can keep it that long!

Bergerac Rouge AOC

This is a generous fruity wine and ideal for lunch and lighter meat dishes. Good Bergerac Rouge will keep for four to five years quite easily. Some will age even longer but I should say that six years is about the limit.

Côtes de Bergerac Rouge AOC

This wine is selected from the best of the vats of the harvest and is bottled on the property. It comes onto the market much later than the Bergerac Rouge AOC and age for a longer period – usually about eight years.

This wine is ideal for rich meat dishes, duck, game and cheeses.

Côtes de Bergerac Moelleux AOC

This is a more delicate sweet wine, ideal for those who don't like the sticky, heavier sweet wines and perfect as an aperitif for those who prefer their white wine not too dry.

Saussignac AOC

This is the second sweet wine AOC of Bergerac and those who specialise in producing it do a great job. There are several to choose from and all are highly recommended. As mentioned before, as from 2005 all Saussignac AOC wine must be from hand-picked grapes. This could bring the price up if the producer has to employ extra pickers. The minimum wage plus insurance can increase the cost of production.

There are pockets of iron deposits scattered around Bergerac and this is evident by the village name of Gageac et Rouillac: rouille being the French word for rust. I'm often asked what the 'ac' at the end of the word means. I can tell you that it means 'belonging to' and Rouillac is a perfect example: land belonging to rust!

Gageac et Rouillac is in the region of Saussignac. There are several British winegrowers here, such as Patricia Atkinson, who specialises in sweet wine, and Richard Doughty, one of the well-known sweet wine and organic/biodynamic wine producers in the region but also one of the best sweet wine producers.

Montravel AOC

This region is on the plateau of the extreme west of the Dordogne and there are about 1,200 hectares of vines.

Montravel Rouge AOC

The red wine from this region has a quality similar to that of Pécharmant and Côtes de Bergerac.

Montravel AOC

This wine is dry and well structured and is most suitable for perch or salmon.

This AOC is becoming more and more important as time goes by, some very fine wines are being produced here, the dry whites and rosés are of particular interest and are worth seeking out.

Perhaps it is because this area is a continuation of the plateau of St Emilion.

Côtes de Montravel AOC

This wine is softer and richer and is superb as an aperitif or accompaniment for fish dishes with a sauce.

Haut-Montravel AOC

This is similar to the sweet wines of Bergerac but not quite as sweet – ideal with melon or blue cheeses.

Bergerac Statistics

The following information has come from the annual reports sent to the producers by the CIVRB. It will give some idea of the production and statistics of the Bergerac wine trade.

The CIVRB controls the production of wine from the time when the vine is planted in the ground to the bottling of the wine. Bergerac alcohol control is:

You may also find the following interesting. These are the wine-sales from 2002 to 2005.

You can make many assumptions from these figures, such as:

Heavier sweet wine sales have gone down and the lighter Moelleux have gone up. There could be two reasons for this:

The price of the heavier sweet wine is expensive.

The fashion for sweet wine drinking seems to be changing as lighter wines are becoming very popular as well as being much more reasonable in price.

The rosé has become much more in demand.

Bergerac Rouge is obviously showing better quality.

Heavier reds are not as well liked as they used to be.

Bergerac has its own Wine Fair

A 'Wine Fair' for holidaymakers is held each year in Sigoules [about ten miles south of Bergerac]. It is always at the same time – the weekend after the celebrations of Jeanne d'Arc.

It was started just over twenty-five years ago by the Council of Sigoules. A huge amount of effort was put into it by all the members. Nowadays, it runs most satisfactorily and is attended by hundreds of visitors.

The Fair takes place in the centre of the little town, and during the weekend all the streets are closed and lined with mainly wine stands but there are other stands displaying the local goodies.

It is a weekend of sampling not only the wine but also the food of the region as several restaurateurs participate. Visitors flock to it, and if you are lucky enough to be staying at the campsite nearby, which has a choice of caravan places, log cabins and even tent places around a huge man-made lake, you are within walking distance of the Fair.

The festivities last the whole weekend and include a dinner dance in the village square plus a 'Spectacular' on the Saturday evening. The Spectacular is always something very special and usually from a show in Paris.

Co-operatives in Bergerac

There are three main ones: Bergerac itself, Sigoules and Monbazillac. The biggest is Monbazillac, mainly because a few years ago it joined up with the co-operative of St Laurent Des Vignes. Of course, Monbazillac is the big name in Bergerac, its history going back to long before Sauternes, as explained elsewhere in the book.

Co-operatives were introduced to help small vineyard owners who didn't have the equipment to make their own wine. As with all things there are advantages and disadvantages. The advantages are that the small vigneron's wine is looked after as from the moment the grapes were picked. He would get paid for his harvest and in return was allowed a huge discount on the price of the wine he bought from the co-operatives.

The disadvantage was that the amount paid for each harvest was very low and all producers were paid the same regardless of the quality, so it wasn't long before the producers with quality grapes started to question the price offered by the co-op. In some cases, the wine was left with the producer until there was no alternative other than to accept the price as they needed empty vats for the following harvest.

It was because of this many of the producers left the co-op and started on their own. Unfortunately, being as small as they are they have great difficulty coping with the market. In the last few years it has become even more complicated because regulations have been changed yet again.

As a producer we no longer have to go rushing around the village, or even the next one, to get papers signed if someone bought wine for transportation. The cessation of this is a great relief. Now the authorities have introduced a register which has to be completed by the end of the month and handed into the authorised office not later than the fifth of the following month.

The register has to give an accurate account of the wine movement during the previous month: the wines sold to the public, to négociants, in bulk, etc. It also has to give a true record of the number of bottles in stock and the wine in vats and barrels. You even have to keep a record of wines for your own consumption and we do it by keeping the capsules from each bottle drunk in the house. In the attic we have wine cartons full of these capsules, just in case.

So every month you carry forward the balance of each item, enter your figures for the present month and balance the new totals.

Bergerac Wines in the USA

Bergerac wines are known in the USA. Several of our vignerons have made inroads into the market but none as pioneering as Alexis Lichine who, after buying his vineyard in the Medoc, took his wines to the USA and did a lot to promote the wines of south-west France over there.

Henry Stuart, a wine producer near Saussignac, was one of the first and he took his wines to Dallas where they are now served on a regional airline. Henry's son has a wine bar in Dallas and the wines of Bergerac are included on his wine list.

Charles Martin recently informed me that he had just been over to San Francisco to introduce the wines of Château La Colline – this I thought was very brave, considering the wine regions just north of there! But it must be accepted that his wines, like many other quality wines of Bergerac, can compete with the wines of California. They are different in character and in price, and from my experience of American visitors to Château Monplaisir they have been very well accepted.

Just recently, a programme on the French Channel 4 was devoted to the ventures of Luc de Conti who has recently spent time in the States marketing his wine. Knowing the price of American quality wines, many of those tasting Luc's wine must have been astounded by the quality and the price of his wines.

Digressing just a little, we have American winemakers in France who are doing a great job. On a recent trip to Burgundy with a group, I organised a tasting with Alex Gambal, an American who got 'hooked' on France and settled down to producing wines in Beaune. What a success story – he is now one of the top winemakers!

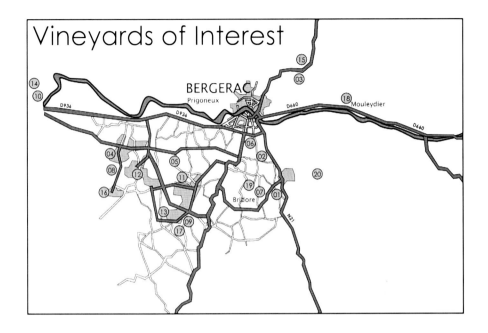

Vineyards of Interest

1. Ancienne Cure

2. Château Bellvue

3. Château Corbiac

4. Château Fayolle

5. Demaine du
   Haut Montlong

6. Château Haut Bernasse

7. Château de la Jaubertie

8. Château K

9. Château La Colline

10. Château de le
    Masburel

11. Château Meyrand
    Lacombe

12. Château Monplaisir

13. Château de Panisseau

14. Château Pique-Segue

15. Château Renaudie

16. Château Richard

17. Château Thenac

18. Château Tiregand

19. Château Tour des
    Gendres

20. Clos des Verdots

Chapter 13

Vineyards of Interest

In the following chapter, I want to introduce you to a few of the vineyards which I find interesting. Some of them are lesser known and you will not see much about them in the wine publicity which is around Bergerac.

When visiting these vineyards whilst preparing to write this book, I was given samples of the wine to taste and then write about it. Unfortunately, most of the wines given to me were too young and I made notes on the labels such as 'Don't open this before 2008'..... etc.

Therefore, I must stress that the following information is given because I hold most of these vineyards in high esteem and would certainly recommend that if you are in Bergerac to visit that you taste the wines they have on offer.

I am not really a sweet wine drinker, but with foie gras, only the best will do! It is for this reason, I have a collection of sweet wines which include a few bottles of Monbazillac – from the vineyards of Chateau Monbazillac itself and some are as old as 1960..... These aren't the oldest because when I was made a member of the Confrerie of Loupiac, I was presented with a bottle of 1926 Loupiac and at the dinner on that occasion we drank 1931 Loupiac – which was delicious...... and I remember finding myself lost for words as its velvetiness slipped down my throat leaving slight hints of tropical fruit……. Imagine, a wine of that age still having flavour!

So in the following selection of favourite vineyards, I should like to start with my favourite Monbazillac producer.

Château Bellevue (2)

Gérard Lajonie
Ste Christophe
24240 Monbazillac.
Tel: 05 53 57 17 96
Fax: 05 53 58 06 46
Email: vignobles-lajonie@libertysurf.frt

A few years ago, some friends of mine wanted to buy a few bottles of Monbazillac so went out tasting sweet wines.

We came to this small vineyard, just south of the airport and tasted each of the selection he had on offer – and there it was... the best Monbazillac I have tasted!

The label had the name "Lajonie" and later I had to do some research.

Before I go any further, I must explain that not all the wines we tasted were of the same quality. The particular vintage chosen was obviously a special one for Monbazillac.

Monsieur Lajonie comes from a long line of wine producers and he bought the property in 1970.

Directions

Leaving the airport, at main road [roué Bergerac to Agen], turn left. A short way [5mins] up on your right you will see the vineyard.

Domaine De L'Ancienne Cure

Christian Roche
Domaine ancienne Cure,
24560 Colombier.
Tel: 05 53 58 27 90
Fax: 05 53 24 83 95
Email: ancienne-cure@wanadoo.fr

When you see the word 'Cure' in France you immediately think of a 'thalassotherapy' centre. These are centres where lots of French people buzz off to in the winter for mud treatments, etc. The majority are found in Brittany and around the Pyrenees.

This 'Cure' is quite different – this is the name of a house where a curator lives. Long ago, the curator did live here – but no longer as it is the home of Monsieur Roche the owner of Domaine de L'Ancienne Cure, and his family.

Those who take the 'Decanter' wine magazine may have seen the picture of Christian in the Bergerac article 2005. He is very proud of this and has the article displayed in the wine shop which seems to be a very busy place in the summer. He employs staff who can converse in English, Dutch, Spanish as well as French.

He exports a lot of his wines to the UK: indeed there was a lorry loading up during my visit.

Mr Roche's parents acquired the property during the forties, selling the grapes to the local Co-op. In 1984/85 Mr Roche took over the vineyard, but it was not until he had invested in buildings and equipment that by 1989 he was able to bottle his wine. He also bought Pécharmant sur pied. By now his chai was fitted with automatic temperature control. Part of the crop is marketed as 'Château Terre Male'.

I asked him if his 12 year old son was interested in the wine trade and his reply was that "he was thinking of other things at the moment".

This is a big problem for families with vineyard; children look at their parents working long hours in the vineyards and the wineries and soon develop the attitude that they don't want to be involved in that type of work when they leave school.

I feel that the only way to encourage younger members of the family into the business is to make it attractive, ie good machinery for doing the hard work, good administration buildings and experienced staff. Alas, this is expensive and not many vignerons are in a position to afford this.

The vineyards are on a slope which runs down to the main road and surrounds the administration building and part of the winery.

Directions

This winery is on the main road from Bergerac to Castillones and Villeneuve sur Lot – a very busy road: the village is called Colombiers. As you leave Bergerac, you will see the water tower on the hill on the right and after this there is a bend in the road. It is on this bend where you will find the vineyard and the premises of Domaine de l'Ancienne Cure.

[Fortunately, there is ample space for parking and turning in the car park.]

Château Corbiac (3)

Mr & Mme Bruno de Durand de Corbiac.

509 rte de Perigueux

24100 Bergerac

Tel: 05 53 57 20 75

Fax: 05 53 67 89 98

Email: corbiac@corbiac.com

Web: www.corbiac.com

The property was acquired in the 16th century. The Durand de Corbiac family has run the vineyard since the 18th century. Antoine Durand, a Protestant and a Bordeaux négociant, was the first to run the vineyard.

In 1864 the vineyard was awarded 'la prime d'honneur' by the administration of Napoleon the Third whose aim was to reward those who pioneered the introduction of agricultural machinery. The Cup figures to this day on the Château wall.

Château Corbiac is perhaps the oldest in the area and is very much associated with the Count of Perigord mentioned at the beginning of this book. In fact, it seems that the family who now live here are descendants of the Count.

This is definitely somewhere to visit in the summer and is so easy to find if you take the road from Bergerac to Perigueux. Within ten minutes you are there with advanced warning because as you drive along the road you cannot miss the majestically standing château on the top of the hill on the right of the road.

As you turn off the road and up the hill, passing a little stream where there is a notice warning you that fishing is strictly private, then passing through woodlands, you eventually arrive at the château set in grounds which would be ideal for a musical evening in the summer.

Alas, the château itself has seen better days and is crumbling in some places. There is a ruin of a pigeonnier which in this region at one time was only to be found in the grounds of the 'elite'. The pigeons' dropping were used as fertiliser – before Fisons came along………

I was taken into the visitors' room and then led through to the kitchen by the mother. Antoine Durand de Corbiac, who has probably taken his name from the first owner of Corbiac, was in the winery but arrived just as his mother had lifted the tablecloth on to a roller for storage.

We talked about the history of Corbiac, Pécharmant and then the wines. Antoine believes that Château Corbiac stands in the original Pécharmant district. It is certainly on the higher ground of the region.

But then, digressing just a little - as you make your way down to the Dordogne river, you have Château Tiregand with what is purported to be the best exposed land in Pécharmant but unfortunately it is so steep that planting vines there would not be economical. You can see this area when driving out of Bergerac on to the road to Sarlat.

In Corbiac's medieval kitchen, huge with a high ceiling, Antoine and I had a conversation about CIVRB, the wine syndicate in Bergerac, and how some improvements are required in their communication skills.

Through frustration, Antoine has designed his own Press Release and sent a copy to as many journalists as possible. The work put into this Press Release should be praised. It gives plenty of information about Corbiac wines, the history of the family and the château and I hope that the journalists to whom he sent it took time to read it!

I feel that this young man has a load of responsibility to carry on his shoulders. His parents aren't getting any younger and it is a fairly large winery to run. As well as this, there is the cost of maintaining the château and the grounds ………

Antoine worked in London for two years. The experience gained working in 'Oddbins' helped him tremendously both with his English and the contacts he made with many people in the wine trade.

After our chat, he invited me to taste Corbiac's new wines……

So we visited the winery.

Two weeks before my visit to Corbiac, I was in Chianti – on another of these 'updating my wine knowledge' courses. It was as gruelling as all the others – in fact, I think even worse! Breakfast at 8.30 am and then on the road, going around vineyards until very late – never having time to return to the hotel to change before dinner. Then as most of these dinners were out of town, it took an age to get back to the hotel and never once did I see the bedroom door before midnight!

On one of the vineyard visits, I noticed that the large screw – an object in the destalking machine - had several of its blades edged with plastic screwed on to the blade. I asked the reason for this – nosey me – and was told that it helped the flow of the grapes through the machine. This was the first time I had witnessed such a thing...... and lo and behold there was the same covering on the blades of the destalking machine in Corbiac!

I asked if Antoine knew what it was for .... he wasn't sure but perhaps that was his father's side of the business. We tasted two of the wines of 2005.

The first was a Merlot on its own: it was quite delicious, fruity, fruity and fruity. The colour was dark as I expected the 2005 Bergerac reds to be as we had such a dry summer – it didn't rain for five months! I swallowed a little and thought to myself "That's my vitamin C for the day!" The second was quite different.

This was a Merlot and Malbec blend. Well, perhaps you don't know – so I'm going to tell you – that Malbec is the grape of Cahors but is also included in the cepage of Bergerac. The wine produced from Malbec in the Cahors region is called 'The black wine' as it is so dark in colour. It can be quite harsh at times and doesn't have a particularly long life. But, when produced in Bergerac – and especially when blended with other grapes - it can enhance the colour and complement the wine.

Well, you can imagine what I found in tasting the second wine – all I had wished for!

A deep, plummy colour and oozing with structure with a balance of fruit and tannin to set your imagination running wild as you started to wonder what it will be like at a later stage -

with a little aging. This is a superb wine – a true quality Pécharmant.

As we left the winery, I noticed in the corner a brand new hydraulic press! I like this type of press, I find it the most efficient, pressing so well that it leaves the dried grape skins like sawdust in your hands. I've seen several just lately – so bang goes the story that they are never used nowadays. I never believed this because even in my early learning days I knew that one was being used in Château Mazarin in Loupiac.

Directions

Leaving Bergerac on the Perigueux road, and just before you come to the village of Lembras, you will see on your right, Château Corbiac, majestically standing on the hillside. The entrance is a little further along the road and the drive up to the Château is most interesting as you wind your way over a little bridge and pass some ruins from medieval times, hence you can witness some of the history of years gone by.

Château Fayolle (4)

SARL Marcassin. [Ringwood Brewery, Hampshire]
24240 Saussignac
Tel: 05 53 74 32 02
Fax: 05 53 74 32 02
Web: www.fayolle.co.uk

Chateau Fayolle once made some of the best wine in Saussignac - it was very well known at one time.

When I brought wine enthusiasts to the Relais de Saussignac to tour the vineyards of Bergerac, we were sometimes short of bedrooms and the manager would phone Fayolle who always helped out by providing accommodation.

Unfortunately, it was during this time that Fayolle was mixed up in some scandal which involved selling Bergerac wine under the Bordeaux AC. I don't know the whole story, all I do know is that two other Bergerac vignerons were involved and for their crime received a prison sentence.

Everyone knew about the quality of Fayolle wines, the producer and his wife were very much respected. The wines were in the high price section of the Relais de Saussignac restaurant's wine list. It didn't take long for deterioration to step in, the producer was sent to prison and because of neglect, the vineyards of Fayolle were ruined and its high quality wines were lost to the market. Years later the vineyard was sold to Ringwood Breweries of Hampshire. I doubt very much if Chateau Fayolle will ever return to its former glory, too many years of production have been lost. And the Chateau has lost its place on the Bergerac ladder of importance.

Well, here's a winery with a completely different approach to producing Bergerac wines.

The very approachable Jeremy Broyd, who manages this estate, was one of the first to be employed at Chateau Monplaisir when David, my husband, took it over.

He stayed only about six months because one day, in the post office in Saussignac, he met the owner of Ringwood Breweries, David Welsh, who had just bought a chateau outside the village, along with the winery and he needed someone to produce the wine. Jeremy Broyd was the ideal person.

Jeremy had moved to the Dordogne a few years previously with his family who had bought a vineyard in Saussignac. Unfortunately the marriage failed -as it often does in these moves to the Dordogne and soon after the vineyard was sold and the parents moved back to the UK. Jeremy stayed on and found work wherever possible, looking after holiday properties during the owner's absence and any other work he could get hold of…….

This is how he came to work at Monplaisir – he knew the work of the vineyard and spoke fluent French – after all, he had helped his parents. David Welsh offered him the job as winemaker at Chateau Fayolle. He couldn't refuse such a good offer even though he enjoyed working for David Baxter at Monplaisir. It wasn't long before he found a helping hand and together they produce the wine of Fayolle.

I have known the wines of Chateau Fayolle for many years since I first started bringing groups to Saussignac. On several occasions I had need of extra rooms because the Relais de Saussignac had only 17 and sometimes one or two were let to others, the owner of Fayolle kindly offered me the extra rooms required.

The wines of Fayolle were majestic – the best in the area. Unfortunately, and I don't know the real story but this is what I interpreted at the time, the owner – with two other producers in the Dordogne were involved in a Bordeaux scandal. The Bordeaux négociant was buying Bergerac wines – bottling as Bordeaux and I gather that the inferior Bordeaux wine went into Bergerac bottles! But this is just what I have heard on the grapevine…

It wasn't long before the authorities found out about this and all involved were sent to prison. The vineyards of Fayolle were left to ruin and they have never recovered. Several years later, Jeremy realised that Fayolle wine would never have the glory of before, times have changed and the competition has changed. But that won't matter to Jeremy because he is in a different business.

David Welsh has a ready market for the wines – he still has to sell it to pubs, restaurants and clubs – but the contact is there. So this is how Jeremy looks at his particular type of wine production.

He visits the UK regularly and, on these visits, makes a point of finding out exactly the type of wine the clients are looking for – then he comes back to Fayolle and produces it – "Just like that".The wines are produced not so much Bergerac style, ie Bergerac Rouge and Cotes de Bergerac Rouge. His red wine is light, fruity – no complexity to it and not produced for ageing. Fermented, spending a reasonable time in the vats then bottled and sent to the UK. He also produces white wines – all from the Semillon grape but in three different styles, Bergerac Sec, Bergerac Sec with ageing and a Sparkling wine. It should be noted that Bergerac is not a sparkling wine region, but one or two producers will send a certain amount of wine for 'methode traditionalle' treatment – I know of one vineyard where this is done in St Emilion.

So this is the new Chateau Fayolle wine and it is certainly worth making a visit there because, although the chateau has not yet been completely restored, you can see a lot of the history of the region – just in the ruins and if you notify Jeremy in advance of your visit you will also be able to taste the new wines.

Directions

LeaveBergeracontheroad to Bordeaux, soon you will come to Gardonne where just at the corner garage on the left, there is a sign to Saussignac. Take this road and before you arrive in Saussignac you will see the sign to Chateau Fayolle.

Tasting

I would like to suggest that you taste the sparkling wine of Fayolle. It is produced with the Semillon grape and is deliciously refreshing. This type of wine is available in Bergerac but is produced elsewhere. The sparkling wine of Fayolle is ideal as an aperitif, Kir Royale or with a rabbit dish.

****It should be noted that Chateau Fayolle has recently been taken over as part of the Ringwood Breweries by Marstons UK.

Château Haut Bernasse (6)

Guy Villette
24240 Monbazillac
Tel: 05 53 58 36 22
Fax: 05 53 61 26 40
Email: contact@hautbernasse.com
Web: www.haut-bernasse.com

Reading up on this property before making the visit, I found out that it had been one of the many sadly neglected by previous owners. A lot of work has been done to build suitable administration premises and expand the main building to make room for stock, etc, but there is still a lot to do and a vast amount of money to be found to do it.

This property was formerly owned by Madame Bouyssy, then acquired in a poor state in 1971 by Monsieur Blais who was responsible for replanting 95% of the vineyard.

The vineyard was then expanded from 6 Ha to the current 20 Ha of which 16 Ha is white.

The chai has a variety of styles, stone, fibreglass and stainless steel but the most interesting item for me was to be found in another room - a hydraulic press. In fact, there are two and I was very pleased to hear that they are still used.

Xavier, the person

Directions

This vineyard isn't difficult to find. Leaving Bergerac on the Eymet road and after passing the Grappe d'Or Restaurant on the right, continue a little further and you will see a sign on the left to Malfourat. Turn into this road and follow it until you arrive at a T junction. Turn right and follow the signs to the winery.

responsible for the winery, explained that this method takes time but the results are good – and I agree with him.

I remember years ago being told during my studies that these presses were no longer used, then I visited Château Mazarin in Loupiac and found one still in use – proving the saying that 'you cannot believe all you read'. Anne Marie of Mazarin always insisted that this method got out more juice than any other machine. I was there one day just when they had finished the pressing and waiting for the barrel shaped container to be opened to find the pressed grapes at the bottom – it looked just like a giant sponge cake and the name the French give this mound of pressed grapes is actually 'CAKE'. I felt the remains and they were just like sawdust – so dry – unbelievable. I thought to myself that the distillery which is authorised to collect all this from the wineries to make commercial alcohol, certainly won't get much alcohol out of this lot. This distillery arrangement is another form of tax which the vineyard has to pay.

Domaine Du Haut Montlong (5)

Alain and Josy Sergenton
Domaine du Hautlong,
24240 Pomport.
Tel: 05 53 58 81 60
Fax: 05 53 58 09 42
Email: sergenton-haut-montlong@wanadoo.fr
Web: www.chambre-bergerac.com

When Alain Sergenton's father, René, bought the property in 1950 it comprised only 6 ha. With his two sons he saw it grow to 17 ha by the time he retired [13 ha white and 4 ha red]. Then Alain took charge and acquired further plots: 6 ha red, then 5 ha more and then 2 ha in Pomport to produce a Monbazillac. Alain revitalised the property adding a chai, inox cuves, temperature control, etc. One of his daughters studied at la Tour Blanche with the aim of continuing the family tradition.

I enjoyed visiting Alain and Josy very much. For years I have been following their progress 'from afar' but in my busy life, never found time to make a visit. When you bring groups to Bergerac, you usually have time to visit two or three vineyards and regrettably, Haut Montlong wasn't ever on my list.

Haut Montlong is situated

Directions

To find this winery, it is best to take the road signed to Mont de Marsan out of Bergerac. Within a few minutes you will pass the Cave Co-operative of Monbazillac. Just after that, on your right, you will see a sign to La Ferriere. Take this road and within a few kilometres you will see a sign on your left to Domaine Du Haut Montlong. This hilly road will take you straight to the vineyard.

high on a hill on a similar level to those of St Emilion and is easy to access from the D14, 3kms east of La Ferriere.

This is a real family business and the history of the family in the wine trade goes back to the time of the Wars of Religion. Alain told me that it was his ancestors who were the winemakers for Chateau Monbazillac during this terrible time.

The winery isn't all that big – they seem a little crammed for space but the views from it over the Dordogne are fantastic. A little further down the road from the winery there are properties on the opposite side of the road. One property belongs to a daughter, another building which is used as an extension to the winery and a third has been converted into a chambre d'hote.

Alain and Josy's two daughters have made their careers in wine, one is an oenologist and the other specializes in marketing. Both are married and the spouses are also in the family wine business. Therefore you have an excellent team of six working together. Although they are in their eighties, Alain's parents are still involved with the business.

There is a superb selection of wines on offer – from basic to haut de gamme a term used for 'top of the range'. To give you some idea, in the Monbazillac range, there are three for you to choose from, the basic, late harvest and hand-picked and late harvest, hand picked and aged in oak. In other words, to suit every taste of those who enjoy Monbazillac. There is a similar selection of Bergerac Sec and Bergerac Rouge, the latter includes a Côtes de Bergerac Rouge.

What interested me most on this visit was a wine which Alain doesn't call a wine because it has only 6% alcohol – though in wine educational terms is wine.

Before going on, I should explain that:

non-alcoholic	0% alcohol
alcohol free	less than 0.5%
dealcoholised wine	less than 0.5%
Low alcohol	0.5% to 1.2%
Reduced alcohol	1.2% to 5.5%

When the reduction in strength is due to dilution, it may not be described as 'reduced alcohol' WSET®

Alain said that he would not like this wine to be included on a wine list and immediately 'big mouth' disagreed with him.

In this day and age, we need wines like this on the Wine List of restaurants. I think it is a psychological need. There is usually one driver at the table, and for him/her to sit with a glass of water – or heaven forbid, a soft drink in a wine glass, it can put the dampers on an evening out. To be able to order a glass of 6% alc wine and drink it without fear of your faculties being dimmed seems rather good to me! So, go ahead Alain – put it on the wine lists of restaurants!

The Sergenton family have won many awards for their wines and the certificates would easily cover the walls of the Salle de Degustation, but there are other items of interest – such as cans of foie gras, paté, and other regional delights - an ideal place to shop for goodies to take back to the UK. For those who visit Bergerac and don't want to visit vineyards, you can buy Alain's produce in Bergerac because he has a small shop or 'garage' as he calls it, near the CIVRB on the rue Recollets down to the port, which is stacked high with wines and conserves and is open from May until the end of September.

You will notice the web site address, www.chambre-bergerac,com – strange for a vineyard – you may think but Domaine du Montlong is not just a vineyard, it also has bedrooms to let for summer visitors.

Château de la Jaubertie (7)

24560 Colombiers.

Tel: 05 53 58 32 11

Fax: 05 53 57 46 22

Situated at an altitude of 170m on a chalky/limestone plateau of 'rendzine', covered in fine clay maintaining humidity, the 33 sections make up a vineyard of 41 ha [101 acres]. In1903 it was listed by Editions Feret as belonging to the Boysson family. Built in the 16th century by an aristocrat for one of his mistresses it is said that 'lo nouste Henric' flirted with Gabrielle d'Estrées: on ne prete qu'aux riches.

Henry Ryman, now happily retired, gave Bergerac wines 'respectability' about 25 years ago. He fulfilled his dream by selling off his stationery stores in the UK and bought Chateau La Jaubertie, near Monbazillac in Bergerac.

Henry, an astute businessman, arrived with his wife Anne and family, cars and animals, not knowing a thing about wine and set out to find a local vineyard manager who, with other workers, started work, replanting the vines where necessary.

Henry invested a great deal of money in machinery and equipment - so much so that it left his finances quite low and when it came to ageing some of his wines in barrels the problem of 'how to pay for the costly barrels' arose. [Nowadays new French oak barrels are priced at over £300 each!].

A prominent nightclub owner in London came to the rescue. The money was borrowed on an agreement that the first wines bottled from the barrels were sold to the Club. Other 'deals' with business people, wine buyers and enthusiasts helped with the funding to get the winery going. It wasn't long before 'Ryman Wines' were in British off licences, restaurants and bars.

He had tremendous publicity, wine writers were continually arriving at the Chateau built for one of the 'royal mistresses' in the 17th century.

When Henry's son, Hugh, returned from Australia where he had followed on his wine studies after Bordeaux University, he became the winemaker. The wines improved dramatically, being produced using New World methods.

Bergerac wines were at last on the British market - although there were two types, ie 'Ryman's' and 'others', that didn't matter. When I made presentations of these wines it was no longer necessary to explain to my audience that Bergerac was not in Jersey but in South West France!

The book 'A Chateau in the Dordogne' by Jeremy Josephs and published by Smith Gryphon in 1995 is still being read and discussed. It was only recently I was asked by an Australian if I had a copy of the book. "Of course, I have" - and lent it to her.

Knowing the family as well as I did, I felt some sadness when I read the book, their family feuds and so on. There was never any mention of the happy times I had witnessed. Henry [or Nick as he is known] spent a lot of time with the visitors I took there for lunch – in fact, he was much admired by many of the ladies…. Also, unknown to many, was the help he gave to other English winemakers

Anne, his wife, once she got out of the kitchen, joined in all the fun. I loved her lunches – typical Dordogne. We had a plate of soup – finishing with the 'Chabrol' [by adding a little wine to the last drop and drinking it – I am told that everyone who visits the Dordogne should do this!!!!] After this we were served with charcuterie and crudités. On the same plate, [we had cleaned it with our bread, because the vinaigrette was so good] Confit du Canard

Directions

Take either the route out of Bergerac to Agen or Monbazillac. The Agen route is well signposted. If you go from Monbazillac, go straight through the little town and follow the signs to Colombiers. You won't go wrong if, after leaving Bergerac, you keep your eye on the hills to the right. In time a water tower will come into view and Château de La Jaubertie is situated right behind it.

was put before us with Pommes Sarladais. Cheese followed – as always in France – then we turned our plate over – as is done in the Dordogne - and prunes soaked in Monbazillac, then cooked were dished up to finish a delightful meal.

We drank the wines of Jaubertie and a great time was had by all.

It is sad to think that this astute businessman, who arrived with wife Anne and family, cars and animals, not knowing a thing about vines or wine had been brave enough to take up such a task – and for the whole thing to end as it did.

He had tremendous publicity – but somehow it all went wrong.

Hugh, his son, now looks after the wines of the Château.

Jaubertie produces a good selection of wines, but my recommendation would the 'Mirabel' which is quite delicious.

Château K (8)

Thor Mowinckel, Fermage [Katharina Mowinckel]

Le Fougueyrat

24240 Saussignac

Tel: 06 72 13 73 17

Fax: 05 53 58 79 60

Email: mowi@wanadoo.fr

I've heard this story somewhere before – but this one - is of a brave young woman.

Katarina came over from Norway to Paris in pursuit of her passion – horse riding. She lived and worked there for nine years and then decided as she was nearing the great age of 30, it was time for her to change direction. She came to the Dordogne to work in a vineyard – the only thing I can find in common with her previous work is outdoor life!

As many of us do, she became passionate about winemaking and enjoyed the five years she spent working with a viticulteur du Bordelais............

Then a property came up for sale – with six hectares of vines. She discussed the vineyard with her mentor who suggested that if her family bought the property he would help her run her own vineyard.

With his guidance, she now has one of the prettiest little wineries I have ever seen. The entrance is decorated with a mass of flowers – in fact so many; I had difficulty finding it as the sign with'Chateau K' was almost hidden. She said that there is a reason for this – she prefers visitors to make an appointment so that she can prepare for their visit – rather than having to be on the premises all the time to receive passers by.

The entrance leads straight into the tasting room with a low ceiling, traditionally furnished and decorated. Then on to the small barrel room with two large barrels for fermentation and ageing. She told me that she was going to change one of the barrels because it was too big [50 hectolitres] and this wouldn't be too expensive to do as the cooper intended to lift off all the fittings and use these on the smaller barrel. The wall in this room has been decorated by an English woman and shows relief work in stone of angels sipping wine – very effective.

In the next area there are a couple of stainless steel tanks which are also used for fermentation.

Like many, she came to the Dordogne with absolutely no knowledge of wine and after only a few years is making a wine that Bergerac should be proud to say is one of theirs.

Her brochure is worth a read, simple, easy and describes the wine and soil – as well as vinification, in a way that everyone will understand.

She produces two types of wine, one which she refers to as the Haut de Gamme – up market and Entre de Gamme – lesser quality.

Directions

It is not the easiest place to find – I tell you that now because if you plan a visit it is better to telephone in advance and Katarina will give you directions and meet you. This is how I had to do it ... after spending ages going around in circles – passing the premises several times.

I asked her why she didn't have the winery better sign-posted and she told me that she didn't want people just dropping in for a tasting as this takes up her valuable time – running the business on her own. She also added that she is quite serious about her wine making and loved to talk about her efforts to people who were truly interested. Well worth finding!

I have tasted both and would recommend that if you're buying to go for the quality wine – there is quite a difference. I was quite impressed with this production.

Château De Masburel (10)

O. and N. Donnan.

33220 Fongueyrolles

Tel: 05 53 24 77 73

Fax: 05 53 24 27 30

Email: chateau-masburel@wanadoo.fr

Web: www. chateau-masburel.com

I have written quite a bit about Olivia, the present owner of Masburel in an earlier chapter. She is one of the modern female winemakers of Bergerac and I admire the work she has done to put Bergerac into the 'quality zone'.

The vineyard has been in existence since 1740 and was created by Jean de Sambellie, the first consul of Ste Foy La Grande and consul to the King of France. His name is visible on the door of the Chateau. Ownership passed onto Mr Loubradou in 1838, then to several owners before the Condet family acquired it. In 1979 Mr Barthoux bought it before being purchased by the Donnans in 1997.

The château – in mixed girondin and périgordin style - was built around 1740 by Sambelli, advisor to the King and first consul of Sainte Foy La Grande. His name is visible on a door of the Château.

In 1838 the property passed into the hands of a wine trader, Pierre Loubradou, and was then split among several owners. In 1903 Le Féret noted production amounted to 10 tonnes of red and 15 tonnes of white [grapes or wine?]. In 1979 Mr Barthoux bought it from the Condet family and went about improving the condition of the vineyard. It was then purchased in 1997 by an English couple, the Donnans.

I'm glad to see that there is a little ungi blanc variety in the vineyard. The majority of vineyards have pulled such vines up. The juice is quite acidic and it is a very important grape in Cognac for making brandy.

I have always thought that some wines of the south west need a little acidity – and this is why the Sauvignon Blanc is so important to the Semillon grape, the latter which can be quite flabby at times and by adding Sauvignon Blanc this can take away the flabbiness.

Someone who has a little Ungi Blanc in the vineyard and can use it properly in the vinification can achieve excellent results.

I had the chance of tasting one or two of the wines of this château and can thoroughly recommend the 'Montravel' which, although dry has a character of its own from the inclusion of the Muscadelle grape.

On the day I opened it we had fish on the menu and horrible memories came flooding back to the time when I had bought quite an expensive bottle of Bergerac Sec for a special fish dish we were having that day. To my shock and horror, it tasted sweet – there had obviously been some experimenting which had gone sadly wrong but I shall tell you that it ruined the lunch! I wish there was something similar to the 'Trade Description Act' in France!

Directions

Now, this is a difficult one – but well worth finding!

Take the road to Ste Foy La Grande – which is on the main road between Bergerac and Bordeaux. The Dordogne River runs through Ste Foy La Grande and the bridge over it is part of the main road.

Once you cross this bridge, you will be on the right bank, immediately, there is a roundabout and on that roundabout you will see a sign to Montpon – follow it – [it is a case of going back on yourself in the direction of Bergerac on the other side of the river!]. Taking great care, within a few seconds, you will come to traffic lights and this is where you turn to the left.

As you climb the hill you will see a sign on the left directing you to Fongueyrolles and after a short drive you will arrive at Château Masburel.

Anyway, in for a penny............. I decided to take a chance with this Montravel which is a dry wine but looked darker yellow than normal – but I put that down to the Muscadelle content. It was delicious and went beautifully with the dish I had prepared.

Château Meyrand Lacombe (11)

Le Meyrand
Pierre and Jessy Lorenzon
La Pouzy
Cuneges
24240 Sigoules
Web: www.meyrand-lacombe.com

This must have been the first vineyard family I met in the Dordogne!

There are many Italians in the Dordogne. The Lorenzon family – along with many others - came over from Italy when France suffered a heavy loss of life during the First World War. The Dordogne had suffered badly and there were very few men left to look after the land. The Government invited Italian farmers to come to the region to look after the land and eventually it became theirs.

At one time this was much resented by the French agriculture people, some Frenchmen became quite jealous of the progress the Italians were making and the better life style they enjoyed because of this. It was silly really because the Italians worked extremely hard and all hours.

One of the barns they owned had been converted into a house for the parents by their two sons, Michel and Pierre, who was already married and lived in another barn nearby which was in an extremely primitive condition.

At that time they had cows and fields - this was their livelihood – apart from money made by the father who was a 'faith healer' – and a very good one!

Not long after this, the sons decided to turn some of the fields into vineyards. Their first effort was undrinkable – a sparkling wine and that idea was soon put on the shelf!

After this disaster they concentrated on dry white wine and red wine. They struggled to get it all going and because of a lack of cash were unable to publicize the wines

In 1983, I received a phone call from one of the sons to say that the family had got enough money together for him to share a stand at the Agricultural Fair in Paris and the red wine presented had won a Gold Medal!

It all changed after that.....

Fortunately, as the sons were the right age they were able to get grants from the government to help with the cost of machinery – and they took full advantage of this. The winery expanded and they were selling more and more wine.

Pierre and Nicole had two children, a girl and boy. The boy was called Jessy – after much searching and a visit to the priest! The reason was that Pierre loved westerns – and sometimes fancied himself as a cowboy. His favourite cowboy was Jessie James. It was decided that their son should be called Jessie, but as you know, Catholics like to name their children after Saints and those from the bible. Nicole had never heard of a St Jessie and went to see the priest one evening. She came back from

Directions

Take the road out of Bergerac to Mont de Marsan. After a couple of kilometres you will climb a hill and at the top you will come to a road junction on the right. There is the restaurant La Grappe d'Or on one side and a little grocery on the other. Turn right here and follow the sign to Cunéges.

You will arrive at a crossroad with closed garage on your right – on the other side [still on your right] a grocery store and bar. Cross the road – keeping both on your right, drive over the 'sleeping policeman' then turn left more or less immediately. It is signposted "Le Meyrand". The Marie and the Church is on your right. Continue down this road for nearly a kilometre then you will start to climb a hill. At the top of the hill – on your right is the winery of Chateau Meyrand Lacombe.

her visit smiling – no, gleaming because the priest had told her that there is a Jessy in the Old Testament!

As time has gone on, the grandparents passed away and the property was shared between Pierre and his brother Michel and sister Jacqueline. The sister didn't want any of the land and Michel the brother wanted to do something else – so arrangements were made that Pierre should take over the vineyards and his son Jessy would be trained to take over – which is just what has happened. At the age of 30, he was running Château Meyrand Lacombe.

The wines are well produced – they always have been. Everything the Lorenzons did was with the word 'quality' in mind. It was said that the vineyards were so well kept because Grandma Marie used to go around them with a vacuum cleaner! I never saw her doing that but she was still working in the vineyards at the age of eighty!

When the Lorenzons first started making wine, they, like the majority of others would sell it to the local co-operative. It broke their hearts to see grapes of such good quality like their quality grapes being thrown in vats with grapes that had come from neglected vineyards.

They also thought that because their grapes were of good quality, the quality should be respected by the Co-operative offering a price to correspond with the quality of the grapes.

It wasn't long before they approached the Co-operative and asked for a better price for their produce – the Co-operative refused and the following year the Lorenzon family started on their own – and never looked back!

Château Monplaisir (12)

Celtic Cousins Ltd.

David Baxter and Helen Gillespie-Peck Baxter

24240 Gageac-Rouillac.

Tel: 05 53 23 93 92

Fax: 05 53 23 93 83

Web: www.wineschoolbergerac.com

            www.gageac-monplaisir.com

Email: vinedab@club-internet.fr

            winewoman@club-internet.fr

Its history is relatively recent, perhaps from early in the 20th century.

There is no great history to the actual château, in fact, the information we have is quite a sad tale. The father of the seller is believed to have been a member of the Resistance and built the château as you see it today by adding to a smaller property. The superb views over the Dordogne valley are to be envied by many. Unfortunately, the son didn't seem to have the same enthusiasm as his father for the estate and over the years deterioration crept in as explained in an earlier chapter. David purchased the château from Mr Coq in 1997.

Directions

From Bergerac, I would recommend that you take the road to Mont de Marsan. After a few minutes, you will pass the Co-operative de Monbazillac and shortly after that you will see a road on the right, directed to La Ferriere. This road runs parallel with the Bergerac-Bordeaux road but is slightly further south. Turn into this road.

The Wine School at Château Monplaisir is, at the present time, one of two International WSET® [Wines and Spirit Education Trust] centres in France. Students come from the UK, USA and France to study for WSET® Certificate at this residential centre.

Short courses are also run in the summer for those who want to learn something of the wines of Bergerac – or even spend a few days studying the wines of Bordeaux.

After about ten kms you will arrive at the crossroads of La Ferriere. Turn left following the sign to Sigoules and Gageac-Rouillac. Not more than 100 metres after this you will see a sign on the right to Gageac-Rouillac; take this road and Monplaisir stands proudly at the top of the hill on the right.

Private wine tours of the South West of France are also organised from here.

Château de Panisseau (13)

A.R.I.C. & Manager S.A.Panisseau.

Château De Panisseau,

24240 Thenac.

Tel: 05 53 58 40 03

Fax: 05 53 58 94 46

In 1932 when a farmer [Monsieur Becker] from the north of France moved to the Dordogne this all changed. He bought Chateau Panisseau, a property which later interested Henry Ryman [joint founder of Ryman Stationers in UK before he bought Chateau de la Jaubertie].

Monsieur Becker wasn't a sweet wine drinker and it didn't take him long to start producing dry white wine.

Chateau Panniseau built around the 13th century and notably the home of Grimmoard Panisseaud, is situated near the villages of Cunèges, Thénac and Sigoules, an important wine growing area of Bergerac. The land is set back from the Dordogne on one of the highest points of the left bank of the river.

Directions

This château is a little trickier to find. Take the road to Mont de Marsan and at the top of the hill there is a road on your right, easily spotted because of the restaurant La Grappe d'Or on the corner. Turn into that road and continue until you come to a small crossroad. There is a sign on the right indicating Cunèges. Take this road, and very soon you will come to another crossroads, turn left. This will bring you to the village of Cunèges and at the crossroads there, continue for 25 metres when you will see a sign to Monbos on your left. Take this road and after approx 2 kms, you will see the sign to Château Panniseau on your right.]

There are two interesting sites on this road – the first is as you climb the hill to

The soil is made up of clay, chalk and limestone - ideal for the Sauvignon as well as the Semillon and Muscadelle grapes. The Chateau is now owned by a Belgian family.

A few years ago, this was a very popular wine on the UK market – it seems to have lost its way.....

Cunèges there is a large house on the hill on the left and it was here that the last royalist was taken to be beheaded. He actually lived in the château further up the hill on the right which is called Le Pouzy and is now owned by Pierre and Jessy Lorenzon of Chateau Meyrand-Lacombe.

The other site is actually after turning left at Cunèges to make your way down the Valley to Château Panisseau. You will pass through a little hamlet called Font du Bernais. I could never understand why it was called this – until one of my passengers, who specialised in the history of France - told me that when the King left Pau to travel to Paris, he passed through this area and stopped for water at the fountain. Before he left, he told the village people that they could call the well 'Font du Bearnais' because this is where the King was born.

Château Pique Segue (14)

Mallard, Philip & Marianne
SNC Château Pique Segue
Ponchapt, 33220 Port Sainte Foy
Tel: 05 53 58 52 52 / 01 39 75 63 36
Fax: 05 53 63 44 97 / 01 39 75 39 69

I have already mentioned Marianne Mallard in my chapter referring to Women in wine in Bergerac – well, this is the Château that she and her husband Philip own in the Dordogne.

I am also very pleased to tell you that her oenologist is no other than Monsieur Daniel Hecquet who once worked for CIVRB and ran courses for vignerons. I attended one of these courses – way back in the late 80s and over the six weeks learned quite a lot about the vineyards of Bergerac. How I wish he was still with CIVRB; the wines of Bergerac would have benefited greatly.

Much of the barrel work is carried out under the eagle eye of M. Hecquet.

This vineyard is now in British hands as in 1903 Panchapt was an independent

Directions

Like Ch. Masburel, this is a difficult one to find – but again worth it!!!

Take the road to Ste Foy La Grande – which is on the main road between Bergerac and Bordeaux. The Dordogne River runs through Ste Foy La Grande and the bridge over it is part of the main road.

Once you cross this bridge, you will be on the right bank, immediately, there is a roundabout and on that roundabout you will see a sign to Montpon – follow it –[it is a case of going back on yourself in the direction of Bergerac on the other side of the river!]. Taking great care, within a few seconds, you commune or village but later in 1990 Philip Mallard,who is British, and his French wife Marianne bought Pique-Segue from M. Sabloux and proceeded to improve it.

will come to traffic lights and this is where you turn to the left.

Keep climbing the hill until you come to a 'fork' in the road on the right hand side. Turn right and this road will lead you to Château Pique-Segue.

Château Renaudie (15)

Yves-Michel and Line Allemagny
Château La Renaudie
46 rte de Perigueux RN21
24100 Lembras
Tel: 05 53 27 05 75
Fax: 05 53 73 37 10
Email: contact@chateaurenaudie.com
Web: www.chateaurenaudie.com

I find the châteaux of Pécharmant most interesting. Of course, this was the first wine region in Bergerac and naturally many châteaux would have been built at that time.

In some ways the contrast between the two châteaux of Lembras is sad. Corbiac, majestic standing on the top of a hill overlooking its vineyards but in desperate need of repair and restoration, in contrast to Renaudie which has been very much restored – still a lot to do but they are getting there. Unfortunately, Renaudie hasn't quite the commanding position of Corbiac and is set back so much that you cannot see it from the road and will not until you have well driven up the hill past one or two other properties.

It was also evident what happens when the original family remains on the property and what happens when the property is sold and resold.

Renaudie has made huge investments in the winery and especially in the barrel department. This is definitely the most modern in Bergerac. The barrels used for fermentation kept my attention for ages....... One had a glass front where you could see quite clearly the wine in the centre of the barrel with the chapeau on top and the sediment lying on the bottom. Some may say this is quite common in high tec wine making but how many of you have seen barrels fitted on curved rollers so that when the wine is fermenting in the barrels, the individual barrels can be rolled to mix the chapeau, wine and sediment, therefore giving more concentration to the wine. And all this is going on in Bergerac.......

I don't know if I have already mentioned it, but I have a great interest in the soil and its contents – I wonder if it goes back to the time when I was a child and one of my favourite games was playing at shops in the back garden. There was an L shaped wall – ideal for my counter and on it I would have a pile of small stones – these were the potatoes, big cod leaves were the cabbage, then the small red seeds which grow on the cod leaf plant were drawn off by being placed between my fingers. This was a special vegetable – and sold well in my little shop. Grass was sold in made up bunches, sticks, etc. Does this sound like a lot of rubbish? Not at all, I was using my imagination which not many children have the chance to do nowadays – but it was obvious I enjoyed what the soil had to offer – including the stones.... And this takes us back to Renaudie.

After the visit to the winery Monsieur Allemagny took me into the house where indoor tastings are carried out. There was little more than the table and a couple of chairs but there was a small glass cabinet and in it was a collection of stones he had found in the ground – some were extremely old and one or two had been shaped into tools for use on the land. I was stunned! Then the 'piece de resistance' came. He handed me a large lump of iron ore which he had found in one of the vineyards. Well, we are always talking about 'pockets of iron in the soil' and 'ferruginous soil', etc and here it was, perfect proof – this visit was so enlightening!

La Renaudie produces 10% of all Pecharmant wines. It is fermented and aged in

Directions

Leaving Bergerac on the Perigueux road, you come to the village of Lembras. Just before the village you have Château Corbiac on your right and just after Lembras, Château Renaudie is on your left. Two completely different châteaux.

oak barrels from Monbazillac.

The result is a beautiful dark ruby red wine with an extremely agreeable nose of rich red fruits and aromas of vanilla.

Château Richard (16)

La Croix Blanche, 24240 Monestier.

Tel:	05 53 58 49 13
Fax:	05 53 58 49 30
Email:	info@chateaurichard.com
Web:	www.chateaurichard.com

Being one of the few Brits here in the 80s, I was often asked to find a holiday home and one of my favourites was near the peacock farm on the way to Saussignac. It was owned by one of the many Italians in the region whose families had been invited by the French government to come and farm the land in the Dordogne because of the great number of Frenchmen who perished in the war. They were given the land free. This particular Italian produced very good traditional wine in his small vineyard but I think he made more profit from letting out his Gite in latter years. On retirement, the property was sold to Richard Doughty and his French mother and British father. That was until recently because just before I contacted Richard to talk about recent developments, I read in the local newspaper that his mother had died in December 2005.

Richard is a dedicated organic winemaker, and for me, makes one of the best Saussignac Liquoroux in the region. It is the one I'm always asked about by my colleagues and only recently, we had a phone call from a friend who was spending his holiday in Scotland and had managed to find a bottle of this superb Saussignac wine.

The history of the vineyard is as follows:

Rabelais extolled the virtues of Monestier wines of which La Croix Blanche was part.

The house was built in the 19th century as part of Château La Tour. In 1903 Edouard Féret wrote about the vineyard then in the hands of Maurice Guy, who later it sold it to the Chouet family who retained it until WWII.

Then it was acquired by Mr. Lapoyade and his brothers –of Italian origin - [Monsieur Andre Ola was the brother I knew] who replanted much of the vineyard, renaming it Domaine de La Malaise. The name [mal-aise] was taken from Monestier hospital which cared for leprosy patients. Leprosy must have been rampant all over the south west so I have written about this in connection with Duras and St Emilion.

Owing to a parachute accident Richard Doughty –of French/English parentage – switched from oceanography/oil to running this vineyard in 1987. His first vintage in 1988 carried the name Château Richard accompanied by a lion on the label relating to 'Richard the Lion Heart'.

Richard was appointed President of the AOC Saussignac in 1994.

Directions

To find this winery, it is best to take the road signed to Mont de Marsan out of Bergerac. Within a few minutes you will pass the Cave Co-operative of Monbazillac. Just after that, on your right, you will see a sign to La Ferriere. Take this road. It's about ten kilometres to La Ferriere and once you get there continue for another kilometre or so. You will then see a sign to Saussignac. Take this road, go through Saussignac and continue on to Monestier. It is on this road that you will find the winery of Richard Doughty.

Château La Colline (9)

Charles Martin
Le Bourg
Château Thénac
24240 Thenac
Tel: 05 53 61 8787 / 06 80246367
Fax: 05 53 617109
Email: charles@la-colline.com
Web: www.chateau-thenac.com

When Henry Ryman's son, Hugh, took over a vineyard in Bordeaux, Charles Martin stepped in as winemaker for Chateau La Jaubertie. A few years later, Jaubertie was sold and Charles moved on to run his own vineyard. The vineyard is not far away from where I lived. One day he phoned, informing me of this and said he was going to concentrate on bringing quality to Bergerac wines. This he has done, his wines sell under the name of Chateau La Colline and can be found easily in UK. His reds are outstanding!

Bergerac wine is always being compared to Bordeaux. I'm not sure that Bergerac did the right thing in so far as not coming under Bordeaux AC in the thirties. There are wines which are very similar because Bergerac wine production is continually improving. The wines no longer lie in the 'shadows of the great cousin, Bordeaux' but can now compete healthily with many of the 'Bordeaux'. In fact, some, aged in oak, are often mistaken for St Emilion!

Directions

This château is another which is a little trickier to find. Take the road to Mont de Marsan and at the top of the hill there is a road on your right, easily spotted because of the restaurant La Grappe d'Or on the corner. Turn into that road and continue following the signs to Sigoules.

Charles is now selling his wines all over the world and during my last chat with him, he was telling me he had just returned from San Francisco and you will see his wines over there if you ever visit!

When you arrive in Sigoules, you will come to a roundabout which connects five roads. [I have been told that this is where the name 'Sigoules' comes from. Sigoules means 'five roads' but I can't remember in which language!]

Take the road signposted to Thenac and from there Château La Colline is well signposted.

Château Thenac (17)

Mr & Ms. Shvidler
Contact: Nadège Bégouin
Advisor: Michael Rolland
Le Bourg
24240 Thenac
Tel: 05 53 61 36 85 / 06 24 96 28 81
Fax: 05 53 58 37 13
Email: nadege.begouin@wanadoo.fr
Web: www.chateau-thenac.com

It must be twenty years since I taught young Tony a little of the English Language – he was then only 12 years of age. Unfortunately, he wasn't interested in learning about anything else other than that connected with engineering. His mother and father, the Brancos, have been the 'caretakers' of Chateau de Thenac for many years.

On my recent visit there, I enquired about Madame Branco and was told she is still there, not only caretaking but working in the vineyards. I thought by now they would have returned to Portugal as many Portuguese do after working in France for a reasonable time.

There have been a few changes at Chateau Thenac – when I used to go there it was owned by a French family who originated from the Dordogne but lived in Paris. Then the chateau was sold to a Swedish family. The big shock came in 2001 when we heard that it had been sold yet again to the owner of the Chelsea football team Mr Abramovich – although the owner of the property hasn't the same name.

Since then, the renovation of the chateau has been going on and it won't be finished for at least another year! Roofs have been put on – and taken off again – because they didn't look right……..

The restoration work, up to now, looks fantastic – if you are able to get in to look around. I had great difficultly because of the many vehicles, portacabins and scaffolding. At last, I found the office and Nadège came out to welcome me and show me around the winery. What a surprise, new equipment – and the very best packed into a small area. Huge vats of stainless steel – apart from one which was much smaller and I noticed that all the handles one would use in working with the VAT were covered with a material and then plastic to protect the wine having any contact with the human hand. This is kosher wine-making and it is done here in Bergerac!

Most of the wine is exported to Russia but a few drops go to the USA, Germany and Britain. I get the impression that as soon as the work on the Chateau is finished they will be building a larger winery.

Directions

This château is another which is a little trickier to find. Take the road to Mont de Marsan and at the top of the hill there is a road on your right, easily spotted because of the restaurant La Grappe d'Or on the corner. Turn into that road and continue following the signs to Sigoules.

When you arrive in Sigoules, you will come to a roundabout which connects five roads. Take the road signposted to Thenac and within minutes you will be there. The Château is on your left as you approach the town – you can't miss it!

It is worth mentioning that when the winery was being refurnished, it was one of Mr Roland's [from Bordeaux] team who came along to advise. Those who have seen the film 'Mondavino' will remember the involvement of Mr Roland in the prestige wineries of France.

I was hoping to mention something about the tasting of the wines at the winery – there wasn't time and also I don't drink and drive. I was given a couple of bottles to taste but with strict instructions that they mustn't be opened for at least another two years................

Château Tour des Gendres (19)

SARL La Julienne, Famille de Conti

Château Tour Des Gendres, 'Les Gendres'

24240 Ribagnac

Tel: 05 53 57 12 43

Fax: 05 53 58 89 49

Email: familledeconti@wanadoo.fr

This vineyard has been in existence since the 12th century as a farm/vineyard. Château Bridoire is situated on gallo-roman remains in magnificent green countryside. Féret in 1903 mentioned it and its owner M. Peyronny. Luc and Martine Conti bought the property in 1981 in order to expand the family farm in Ribagnac. With his brother, Jean, they set about modernising the long abandoned 22 ha [54 acres] vineyard and the first bottles appeared in1987.

Three years on, cousin Francis joined the team adding some hectares of St Julien d'Eymet. Then SCEA de Conti was set up. Luc de Conti believes 80% of the effort must be devoted to the soil and the vines and only 20% in the chais although if you visit his vineyard it is worth taking notice of his barrel ageing techniques

I was introduced to his wines in 1987/88. One of my friends, who is quite a wine enthusiast and lived near the Conti vineyard, brought a bottle to dinner. My friend told me that Luc de Conti was going to be the best wine producer in Bergerac and his were 'outstanding'. I waited with impatience to taste this consecrated wine and I must say I was most impressed. Of course, what I must stress is that at that time the quality of Bergerac wines had not improved a great deal so someone making a decent wine would naturally come to the fore and this white wine of Conti certainly showed promise of the future.

Much later, I tried one of his Bergerac Rouge wines, and this was really quite something – deep and concentrated in colour, loads of body, well balanced – and a reasonable amount of sediment left in the finished bottle!   Again, I was impressed…….

Luc de Conti was one of the first of this new generation of winemakers in Bergerac – and I suppose his experience has helped many of the 'up and coming' others who are now proving that Bergerac wines are quality wines.

His wines are very popular in the UK, in fact restaurants and good wine suppliers stocking Bergerac wines will certainly have Conti's at the top of the list.

Clos Des Verdots (20)

GFA des Verdots

Manager GAEC Fourtout et fils

Les Verdots,

24560 Conne de Labarde

Tel: 05 53 58 34 31

Fax: 05 53 57 82 00

Email: fourtout@terre-net.fr

If I was asked to take a group to a Bergerac vineyard – this is the one I would choose.

The writer Edouard Féret made a reference to 'Verdeau' as it was then known in 1903. The Fourtout family - originally from St Emilion – have made wine for five generations.

In 1962 the family built their first cement vats for their wine. By 1972 they had made their first commercial sales in bottles. In 1991 son David Fourtout rejoined the family business. Each generation arrived with new ideas. For example, a newly introduced Cotes de Bergerac Red aged in oak barrels won a Gold medal in Paris in 1991. 1997 saw a major project underway with the erection of a two storey building to welcome customers and to store both barrels and bottles in a cellar 6-7 metres underground.

After my visit to this vineyard, I had a truly restless night. I woke up several times marvelling on what I had seen.

I have always been very interested in viticulture and what the roots of the vine get up to way down in the ground. I may sound quite mad to some people – but that's the way I am.

For years, I have been explaining to students how the roots of the vines go down in search for water. They can travel far through bedrock till they eventually arrive at the water table level. They bring back the water into the grape but also collect minerals from the rocks in the ground – and this is what helps to make good wine. That is in very simple terms.

In many of the hundreds of vineyards I have visited, I have

seen examples of what is below the top soil - exhibited in glass cases etc. but what I witnessed at Verdot is something I have dreamt of seeing for many years.

David Fourtout followed studies in farming. His father wanted him to go into the vineyard and work with him but David refused because he felt he had a contact with animals which he enjoyed and there was no comparison in looking after grapes!

Later he succumbed and he and his father developed a winery – a winery of the future for Bergerac.

The family vineyard was operated from the centre of the village of Conne La Barde for 32 years. David's mother told me that it had been hard work – never having room in which to work or store wine. They could have never considered further development where they were.

David and his father took advice and fortunately, a very good friend who was once the cellar master of Lafitte Rothschild wineries, pointed David in the right direction.

In 1992, after David joined the family business, things started to happen. The first change was that a new winery was built just outside the village in the heart of the vineyards.

It looks like a huge, high barn with glass doors and in front of it are good parking facilities with each car bay named after a grape. [I had parked in Cabernet Franc on my visit there.]

As I walked through the glass doors a mass of space confronted me. Huge light oak pillars held up a massive, beamed ceiling and roof. The reception desk – displaying the selection of wines produced in the vineyard - looked miniature in all this space. There are a couple of tables, one holding a selection of wine journals and books and the other had four chairs around it – obviously for discussion. Apart from that, it is all space.

At the end of this monstrous 'barn', an area has been divided and behind the glass partition the wines which have been brought in from storage are packed into cartons, loaded on to palloxes ready for transporting.

With the building being so high, a small area has been constructed to accommodate visitors, wine buyers and others. There are three chambre d'hotes and a kitchen.

Then it all happened; David led me through a door and down some cement stairs – often seen in wineries. "We are going to visit the stockroom," he told me. The door opened and there we were in the bowels of the earth! He went on to explain that when he and his father decided to construct this building in farming land, they decided to follow the engineer's advice to excavate and build a massive stockroom underground. This was a tremendous undertaking and the cost only brought a sigh and closed eyes when I mentioned it………

It is, on the whole, a concrete tank underground. But, and this is the biggest BUT I shall ever use, all around the walls were large round holes to view the foundations on which the vines grow. I stood in wonderment, there before me was what I had wanted to see all my wine life! The calcaire and argilo glistening with minerals and I know that all the roots of the vines above would in time penetrate through this to reach the water level. How wonderful! As I was led around – in a complete daze, I was then shown a couple of holes in the floors which had been created to show – guess what? The water level the roots would be seeking. It was breathtaking!

"Come down to earth Helen," I heard myself telling myself. Then David explained what had happened.

When they had started excavating, it wasn't long before they realised that they were 'digging' near and under the small river Verdot which is a tributary of the Dordogne – meandering south and around the area which had just been excavated!

Now you can understand why I had a restless night!

I feel that this project which has taken years and lots of hard work for father and son – must be one of the greatest gifts a son could give his parents. The pride they must have in what they see before them.

I too am proud of what he has achieved, in fact, I would go further and say that although he hasn't the knowledge of some of my top wine students, I could relate to him as teacher/student. He is passionate about what he has done and what he is doing.

The story doesn't finish here. We then went over to the VAT room where I had envisaged what it would be like from the literature I had read. The VATs, designed by David, are wide at the bottom and narrow at the top. This is simply to get more concentration. As the 'chapeau' rises to the top – it has less space and crams together to reach the summit – all clever stuff.

David informed me that he looks upon the Vat-room as his 'kitchen' – ie bringing in good produce and preparing it to be served to the public! Yes, it all makes good sense.

I intend to make sure that educational bodies in the UK know about this vineyard and where possible arrange for students to visit it– then the students won't have to wait as long as I did to see such an excellent explanation of viticulture.

Directions

To get to this vineyard is not too difficult. You have to follow the road to Eymet from Bergerac and keep your eyes open for a sign to Conne de Labarde. The village is about 3 km down the road and just as you leave the village you will see the Maire on your left and the village hall on your right. Turn right there and then right again and follow the signs to Clos de Verdot.

I managed to have a little chat with Madame Fourtout who told me that they were able to hold functions on the premises, but of course, caterers were brought in for those occasions. We talked about the dry weather and how many of the trees around were dying due to the lack of rain. She was absolutely astounded when I said sadly that I didn't expect to be having any Cepes this year – as it had been so dry. She looked at me and said "Where do you come from?" I told her Scotland. "Oh well – that's different! I have never met any English who like cepes. Have you ever had any of the very special ones – with dark brown tops?" I told her I had and she seemed very pleased that I was conversant with the local delicacies.

Château Des Vigiers

SCEA de la Font du Roc
Château Des Vigiers,
24240 Monestier.
Tel: 05 53 61 50 30 (Bureau)
Fax: 05 53 61 50 20

The Chateau was the handiwork of Jean Vigier, a royal judge in Sainte Foy La Grande, starting in 1597. His daughter Marguerite de Vigier saw the finished product around 1620, adding a dovecote which still stands today.

Wine was being produced here in 1903 as Edouard Féret referred to Vigiers as "then producing 50 tonneaux of red wine and 10 of white wine".

In 1989 a Swedish company, represented by the late Mr Petersson, bought the property. He completely restored the building and turned it into a four star country hotel with two restaurants and an 18 hole golf course.

Mr Petersson and I had a mutual friend, Nansi Poirel. Not long after he started work on Vigiers, there was a nasty road accident and one of his staff was killed. The dead girl was an American, a friend of both Mr Petersson's and Nansi's family. Nansi was asked by the American family to visit Vigier and I was invited to accompany her.

We were shown all around by Mrs Petersson, the lovely Fresco Restaurant, the bedrooms which had been individually designed in different French royal periods. So regal!

It is now seen as the major

Directions

From the Bordeaux/ Bergerac road near St Foy La Grande, Château de Vigiers is well signposted. You will turn south at St Foy La Grande and follow the road to Eymet.]

Golf and Country Club in the region with golfers coming from all over the world. Additionally, houses have been constructed on the premises and sold to golf enthusiasts.

There is a 32 ha vineyard attached. The wines are available in the restaurant and in shops in Bergerac. I wouldn't include these wines in my list of quality wines of Bergerac wines, they seem to lack something of which I am not sure, but they are very acceptable as a lighter type of Bergerac wine and Vigiers is a pleasure to visit.

Château Tiregand (18)

Comtesse F de Saint-Exupéry

24100 Creysse

Tel: 05 53 23 21 08

Fax   05 53 22 58 49

The most important factor to make good wine is to have well positioned vineyards, ie: slopes, drainage, exposure, etc. That is what I believe.......

The best piece of land in Bergerac for planting vines is on the Pecharmant Tiregand estate. It is a beautiful gentle slope, facing south and can be seen from the main road as you drive along in the direction of Sarlat; but vines have never been planted there. On one of my many visits, I asked Francois-Xavier why this was?????

His reply was most interesting and it helped me to understand the economics of Bergerac wine which I hadn't fully understood before. He explained that to plant and care for vines on this section would not be financially beneficial.

Bergerac wines at the moment are very under-priced and the truth is that as long as they remain a country wine of Bordeaux in the eyes of the world, there will be no change.

Tiregand make one of the best red wines in Bergerac, excellent claret-style wine with ripe blackcurrant fruit and fine grained tannins - comparable in quality to many of the good Bordeaux and it sells at a very reasonable price – because there is no choice, there is a ceiling on Bergerac wine prices.

If Francois-Xavier went into production on the piece of land I am referring to, he would create a wine of exceptional quality but he would never be able to recover the cost involved in the production.

A visit to this estate is worthwhile. Driving through the grounds gives you some idea of the grandeur of Bergerac wine estates of the past. A beautiful chateau, which is no longer habitable because the termites have taken over, set in rolling parkland and quiet woodland. When you finally arrive at the winery you will be greeted and if an appointment has been made someone will be there to show you around.

Directions

From Bergerac and just before Creysse, there is a turn off on the left – under a railway bridge – which is signposted 'Tiregand' This will take you on to the estate.

On one visit when I was doing a programme for Radio Devon, we were told about the family - related to the famous author and aviator, the connections in Bordeaux and the history of the winery itself – where there is still evidence of the times of war in the chais where Fraancois-Xavier matures his red in old barrels from Mouton-Rothschild.

A note............

Edouard Féret

There are several references to Edouard Féret and you may be confused. Edouard Féret was the original author of what we in the wine world call 'The Bordeaux Bible' which gives detailed information of every chateau in the region. He obviously wrote many other wine books.......

Chapter 14

Restaurants

The Restaurants of Bergerac and around.

Because of my interest in food and wine, for me, there is no better place to live in France – the Dordogne is one of the top gastronomic regions of the country with wine which is underestimated and under-priced. As well as this, the climate is most agreeable – warm summers with mainly night rainfalls during the summer offering green luscious scenery – without the dryness you can experience further south.

As Philip Oyler said, the richest and poorest region in France – and it is the richness that we are able to enjoy.

So let me now take you on a tour of the restaurants of Bergerac.

As far as reservations go, you will most likely be accepted without reservation out of season, but in July and August these restaurants get booked up very quickly so my advice is to make the reservation as soon as possible.

Lunchtime in Bergerac

You will find quite a few Pub Restaurants and the like in the centre of Bergerac but two in particular stand out for me.

The first is 'Le Bureau' which is more or less opposite the Cathédrale Notre Dame, in the main street. This is very much like an English pub inside, a long bar on one side and tables on the other. In the summer, the seating stretches out onto the pavement where a wooden platform has been placed, decorated with lamps and flowers. From here you can watch the tourists meandering by – enjoying the ambience of this market town which has suddenly taken off since the conception of cheap flights to the area.

There is an excellent selection of lunchtime 'plates' - with both French and British/American dishes. The service is also good, with very little waiting around; I feel there is a British influence in the management.

The second restaurant is at the other end of the main street, opposite the Palais de Justice – obviously where the restaurant took its name!!!!

This is smaller, and a great favourite of the local business people who work around the Place de la République. This Square is the main 'hub' of office workers, including dentists, doctors and solicitors. The Tourist Office is also in this Square.

On one occasion, when Flybe representatives came to Château Monplaisir to discuss the possibility of including my wine courses in a programme they were planning, we finished off the meeting with a visit to the Tourist Office. The Director kindly invited us to lunch at Le Palais.

During our conversation, he talked a little about the restaurant and said that the Chef specialised in Tuna fish. With this recommendation, we all had the same plate....Grilled Tuna fish with vegetables. It was superb and I was impressed with the quality of the fish.

These restaurants are ideal when you don't want to waste too much time at lunch – although, I must add that, apart from the

Post Office, most shops close for the usual '2 ½ hours' break'

I think the best example I can give you of this is of one of the supermarkets on the road to Perigueux. On one side of the street, there is the main part and on the other is the 'bricolage', paint, plumbing, garden furniture, car accessories, decorating, etc.

Outside the bricolage, there is a huge display of goods of the day, ie, in the summer, garden furniture, barbeques, flowers and garden tools. In the winter, wood fires and other heaters and anything related to the colder months.

Just before 12 noon, several of the staff come out of the shop and take all the display into the entrance part of the shop – then lock up. This takes roughly 15 minutes. After lunch, when the staff return, you have to wait until the display is then transferred from the entrance inside the shop to the outside patio.

Every time I see this, I can see imaginary flashes with the words 'work study' written on them, running across my eyes. Have they never heard of staggered lunch breaks?

I am pleased to say that things are changing; on a recent visit to town, I did find one or two little boutiques open – which proves to me that it has suddenly dawned on them that more money can be made by opening all day and the British enjoy shopping during lunchtime.

The following list is of restaurants I visit regularly:

Tour des Vents

Chef: Marie Rougier
Moulin de Malfourat
24100 Monbazillac
Tel: 05 53 58 30 10
Fax: 05 53 58 30 55
Email: moulin.malfourat@wanadoo.fr
Web: www.tourdesvents.com

As mentioned in another part of this book, Sunday was a very special day of eating a huge lunch and then taking a walk afterwards to get some exercise. Some Sunday afternoons we would venture up to the Hall of the Moulin de Malfourat. Once we had managed to park, because the place was always crowded and before going in, we would spend some time admiring the wonderful view from the top of the Moulin. After the climb we would go into the little café below and have an Orangina – they didn't sell much more. Later we made our way into the large hall next door. There was a stage at one end with the likes I have never seen before – or ever again. It was a miniature French ensemble fully automatic. The keys of the accordion, trumpet, piano etc were all playing furiously, the drums were being beaten by drumsticks and the music blared out in true French tradition and the people danced and danced and danced……..

These people were the regulars, they went every week and the dressing up was incredible. They were mainly people who worked in the vineyards and fields around and the only clothes you ever saw them in during the day were green or blue overalls. Madame Lorenzon, a neighbour of mine at that time, told me she made her two sons wear a different colour so that she could recognise them from afar in the vineyards. When the weekend arrived the men would wear their best shirt – even though it was a bit tight around the middle. The ladies brought out their lovely frocks and shoes and all this was on view for those of us who sat in groups at the tables set out down the two sides of the hall. Madame Lorenzon also told me that this is where the divorced people come to find a partner! It was a hoot....

I didn't go again for many years. Then one day, after hearing for some time about this very good restaurant – but never having time to go there accepted a kind offer from some of our friends. Jacqui said that she could never remember how to find the place but she knew it was somewhere in the vicinity of Monbazillac. So we made our way past the Chateau and into the village. She didn't recognise any of this and in the end, I asked someone who gave me some weird and wonderful directions. It wasn't until we were getting nearer that it dawned on me where we were heading......Nowhere else than the little café below the Moulin – where crepes were made and I used to buy the Orangina!

The café had been extended inside and where we used to park the car, had been closed off, walled and tables set out with lights and little bushes. The owners had even cut into the side of the hill in front of the Moulin to give a couple of terraces for tables to be set out. What a conversion!

Dinner was very good and the service reminded me of the time I used to teach in hotel management and have lunch in the college restaurant. In fact, I know there is a similar type of college in Bergerac and feel that some of these waiters were from there.

I made up my mind that this would be one of the restaurants I would include in my new book and wrote to Marie Rougier to ask if it was possible to visit her.

She was quite surprised when I said that we had already visited the restaurant and I had noticed that several of her staff looked as if they were at a training college

Directions

The restaurant is easy to find. Taking the road to Eymet from Bergerac, it isn't long before you arrive at the top of the hill where there is a road leading off to the right with a restaurant on the corner called La Grappe d'Or. Just continue past this and take the first turning after on your left. You'll see the Tour de Vent on your left.

– and followed by explaining that one of my many educational jobs was preparing hotel management for the WSET exams at a very good college in Devon. She was most interested and added that it is a pity that there isn't a class for sommeliers in Bergerac. Oh dear! And I say no more……..

I informed her about my trips to Malfourat many years ago and she laughed – "That was when I used to help my mother in the vineyard [on the sloping hill in front of the restaurant]. At that time I was an accountant/book-keeper in Bergerac and my husband was an electrician."

She followed on by telling me how at each vendange, she and her mother would work diligently in the vineyard and on one of these occasions, she suggested to her mother that she should extend the Creperie and have a restaurant.

This is just what has happened, and now, as explained to me, she no longer cooks at home but in her restaurant – and she is doing a fine job!

La Grappe d'Or

Le Peyrat
24240 Monbazillac
Tel: 05 53 61 17 58
Fax: 05 53 61 71 85

This restaurant, as mentioned at the beginning of the book, was one of the first Bergerac restaurants I visited.

The food was always superb and the sauces which accompanied the fish and meat were very, very special.

The restaurant was very traditional, the tables were beautifully set in white linen and silver and furniture looked as if it had been bought out of an up-market antique shop. I shall always remember the large grand piano in the middle of the restaurant – spelling out 'elegance' as soon as you enter. The waiters were dressed in quite snazzy grey Italian suits and someone had trained them extremely well in the art of 'serving at table'.

At that time, the restaurant would close for a couple of months – during which time duck, vegetables, paté and sauces would be prepared for the season. This was quite an operation.

Unfortunately, there were marital problems and the restaurant changed hands several times after that – never returning to its former glory; but then, times change.

I have to be very honest and say that after that time, my visits to this restaurant became infrequent but in recent years I have heard very flattering tales of the restaurant – the main one being that it was "great value

Directions

The restaurant is easy to find. Taking the road to Eymet from Bergerac [signposted Mont de Marsan], it isn't long before you arrive at the top of the hill where there is a road leading off to the right and the restaurant on the corner is La Grappe d'Or.

for money".

We had an Australian family staying with us last year and on arrival I gave them a list of restaurants in Bergerac. They tried each one listed and made comments on their visits.

The Grappe d'Or was their favourite and the one they most frequently visited. They explained that there was so much food offered that the day of the evening they intended going there – lunch would not be taken!!!!!!

L'Imparfait

Chef: Olivier Gineste
Rue Fontaines
24100 Bergerac
Tel: 05 53 57 47 92
Fax: 05 53 57 89 13
Email: reservatins@imparfait.com
Web: Imparfait.com

I have dined in this restaurant for over twenty years; at first when shopping in Bergerac, it would always be at lunchtime. It wasn't anything special, but the atmosphere was cosy.

At that time most of the cooking was done on the fire and in the winter months this was particularly warming – in many ways. It was a set menu and the usual pichet of wine would be put on the table as soon as you made your order.

This is when I reflected greatly on why the pichet of wine on the table was always red – if you wanted white, you had to order it – and it was always more expensive. With my studies of this I found out that the French look upon a glass of red wine with lunch as helping the digestion of the food and giving your body lots of minerals. I say to that - as long as you know where the wine comes from because my first lesson was always drink pure wine [from the vineyard] – you will add ten years on to your life – other wines will take ten years off!

Anyway back to these lovely little lunches. It was usually a choice of steak/frites, steak haché/frites, etc. Bread and a pichet of water was also brought over – without having to ask for it! There was no need to rush – it is not expected in France – just take your time have a nice long discussion on the subject of the day which was usually what you had bought in the shops – or what you were thinking of going back to have another look at! The cost of this type of lunch was extremely reasonable.

Then there was a long break before I visited the restaurant again but when I did I noticed immediately the great difference. More property around had been bought – and the old fireplace where all the grilling used to be done had been renovated and was decorated with flowers.

I then took a look around – to find out where the cooking was done and behind the restaurant was a brand new kitchen – with ultra modern fittings. What a change! "This restaurant has gone up-market," I said to myself.

L'Imparfait specializes in fish dishes and every evening there is a different 'catch of the day' - as well as two set menus specialising in the traditional Perigordin dishes finishing with a delightful dessert which even tempts

Directions

The best thing to do is to park your car at the Port on the cobblestones – [I am told the first to be laid in France]. It was at this Port where the wine barrels were brought to be put on ships which took the cargo up to Libourne.

Back to car parking!

Once you have parked the car, come out of the Port and facing you is the building belonging to CIVRB. At the side of the building, there is a narrow street which leads up to a square - where you will see the original "Cyrano de Bergerac" and also signs to the different restaurants in the area.

ME – someone who is not a great pudding fan!

The wines are local and a good selection – in which I am happy to say the wines of Château Monplaisir are included.

At this point, digressing just a little more, I should tell you that the best fish shop in the Dordogne is to be found in Bergerac. At first it was a small corner shop but later moved into much larger premises, still in the old part of town. The selection of fish is amazing...... ....

L'Enfance du Lard

Chef: Michael Barnes-Wortley
Cadre du XIIe Siecle,
Place Pelissiere,
Vieux Quartier
24240 Bergerac
Tel: 05 53 57 52 88
Email: lenfancedelard@yahoo.fr
Web: l'enfancedulard.com

This is another of my favourite restaurants in Bergerac, it is so cosy and intimate. You feel 'chez nous' immediately you walk into the small dining room. There are only six tables so it is necessary to book. It is very busy in the summer and has a regular clientele.

The windows look out onto the Square which is towered over by the façade of the Church of St Jacques. The new statue of Cyrano is nearby.

This Square in the summer is a delightful venue, covered in parasols which shelter the clients from the sun.These parasols are supplied by the restaurants as the volume of visitors increases and necessitates seating to be spread out into the Square.

There is always some evening activity in the Square during the summer – mainly musical evenings such as jazz, country or pop.

It's run by an Englishman Michael Barnes-Wortley and a Frenchman Andre Morant who have made this restaurant one of the most popular in Bergerac.

There are certain points I have when planning to dine out:

Good local fresh food
Ambience
Good service
Local wine list
Affordable pricing

This restaurant offers all the above and it should be noted that this is one of the few which are open all the year round. The menu, at the time of writing this book is around 26 euros – giving you choices for each of the three courses. The selection ranges from the local delights such as duck, foie gras, etc to the more traditional beef and pork and chicken.

The food is very good – in fact my husband says that the best pork dish he has ever tasted was at L'Enfance du Lard. I remember the occasion very well and I had more or less the same menu; the filet of pork had been grilled on vines and the flavour came right through the meat. The pork wasn't over-cooked, in fact it was slightly rose in the centre. The tenderness of the meat was something to experience.

Directions

The best thing to do is to park your car at the Port.

Once you have parked the car, come out of the Port and facing you is the building belonging to CIVRB. At the side of the building, there is a narrow street which leads up to a square - where you will see the original 'Cyrano de Bergerac' and also signs to the different restaurants in the area.

Continue through this square and you will come to another – which is dominated by the Church of St Jacques.

Opposite the church you will see some buildings and the restaurant L'Enfance du Lard is in one of these buildings.

Digressing once again, I watched a cookery programme recently when one of our prominent chefs said that the British overcook pork – that is because we live in fear of it being underdone and making us ill......... Since then, I have kept this information in mind and have to agree that pork which is cooked – without overcooking - is succulent and delicious.

Back to the restaurant..... When we visited the restaurant just recently with friends of ours, on entering the establishment I allowed my imagination to take over [which is not difficult for me!].

The large entrance door [which must be the original] opens up into a dark long corridor, high ceiling - with a spiral staircase at the end of it. The staircase winds up into the restaurant which has six tables placed comfortably around the room.

Separating the original stone fireplace, where the grilling is done on vines, from the rest of the room is the display cabinet of cheeses and desserts to complete your meal.

The dining-room is medieval in style and the walls are interestingly decorated with items of many years ago – in fact, sitting in such a setting, I feel that at any moment Cyrano de Bergerac with his large nose and flowing long black curls, dressed in his colourful attire and flowing cloak will enter the room – preparing to hand over his plumed hat to the waiter – and then be directed to my table!!!! .

For many of us who have lived in Bergerac for a long time, Cyrano has become part of our lives! Dining in this restaurant will take you back to the past.....

Le Poivre et Sel

Chef: Jean Charrol

11 rue de l'Ancien Pont

24100 Bergerac

Tel: 05 53 27 02 30

Email: jean.charrol@wanadoo.fr

Web: Le Poivre et Sel Bergerac.com

This is a good restaurant to visit in the summer both for lunch and dinner.   There is a warm ambience and during this period, the tables are outside in a little square opposite the restaurant itself. The food is very good – my only complaint would be that the servings are too large!

The street running between the main restaurant and the terrace is one of the oldest in Bergerac – leading from the original bridge to the monastery [CIVRB] – which was all that Bergerac had to offer in the 12th century.

Like other restaurants, they specialise in the local gourmet delights and you have a choice of set menus which are extremely good value or a la carte.

The wines are mainly of Bergerac and are priced to suit the average tourists' pocket.

The restaurant is in one of the oldest streets of the town – in fact, it is one which led onto the original bridge across the Dordogne in the Middle Ages. On this street, you will also find the Tobacco Museum and quaint small shops.

Once you have parked the car at the Port, come out of the parking and facing you is the building belonging to CIVRB. At the side of the building, there is a narrow street which leads up to a square - where you will see the original 'Cyrano de Bergerac' and also signs to the different restaurants in the area.

It is one of these signs which will direct you to the restaurant. When you enter the street, you will see a tearoom, creperie, etc but continue further on and you will come to the restaurant on your left. The 'open-air' part of the restaurant is on your right.

Le Treuil

12 Quai Salvette
24100 Bergerac
Tel: 05 53 57 60 11
Fax: 05 53 74 19 97

This restaurant overlooks the Port and is a great favourite for national celebration nights – especially 14 July, Jeanne d'Arc - when there is a firework display.

The food is good with a reasonable selection of both local gastronomic and other French dishes. There is a very friendly atmosphere and it is popular with the British people.

The only complaint I would have about this restaurant is space. On each occasion I have visited, it has been a Saturday evening – which is always busy and I got the impression that an extra table may have been added to the room as I felt rather crammed. But what you have to bear in mind is that this restaurant is very popular with both tourists as well as residents and is likely to be full to capacity during the season.

Relais de Monestier

Le Bourg

24240 Monestier

Tel: 05 53 57 08 29

This is a small restaurant in the heart of the vineyards of Saussignac AOC.

Take the road to Saussignac then drive straight through the village. Within a couple of kilometres you will arrive at Monestier. You will see the church on your left and the restaurant is just before it.

This is one of the village restaurants I admire very much. The council own the restaurant and subsidise it. It is run by a young chef and his wife. There have been three such couples in recent years. The first – not nearly as good as the second but unfortunately the second chef, a young man, died - and then the third couple took over. They have been running it for two or three years and making a success of it – I hope they stay

There has been a great deal of effort put in by this recent couple – even to the extent of building a new, very pleasant dining room and parasol terrace for summer dining.

The food is exceptionally good for this type of restaurant, it is obvious the chef takes a great pride in his work – the presentation of each interesting dish is superb.

Sometimes, there is a set menu – we have been on a couple of Sundays when this has been the case and enjoyed not having to choose and being pleasantly surprised with each plate put before us.

The wine list is also good – it is obvious that the wife knows something about wines – as the wine list could be described as good quality local wines.

La Pizzeria

Route de Bergerac
Gardonne
Tel: 05 53 27 99 60

West of Bergerac, about 12 km, there is a pizzeria owned by an Italian.

I'm not a pizza person and wouldn't dream of ordering one – except in this restaurant. My preferred pizza is the 'Gardonnaise' – a topping of ham, cheese, onions and fresh cream – very much like a Tart Flambé from Alsace – but about six times as large!

The restaurant is a great favourite in the summer for locals and tourists. Although the restaurant itself is small, there is a huge sitting area out the back and from time to time musical evenings are arranged.

As well as pizzas which are cooked in a traditional round brick oven, there are other Italian dishes accompanied by salads and large chips – which the children love…….. These delights can be followed by one of the many ice-cream desserts listed on a special dessert menu.   Prices are extremely reasonable.

Booking in summer is advisable.

Directions

Leave Bergerac en route to Bordeaux. Gardonne is about 15 mins drive and when you arrive in the village [which the main road runs through], look out for the Pharmacy sign on your right. Just after this is the Pizzeria and before the restaurant is a turning off on the right into the parking behind the restaurant.

Le Cafeteria at Le Clerc

Le Cavaille
24100 Bergerac

[Bus service from centre of town]

Everybody enjoys shopping in the Dordogne and most people take pleasure in having a walk around Le Clerc – the biggest super-market in Bergerac situated at La Cavielle – just west of Bergerac.

The Cafeteria here is very good with an excellent choice of hors d'œuvres, main dishes and desserts at a very reasonable price. Every day there is a roast and they are exceptionally generous with the servings!

Two important tips:

Try to arrive immediately at midi – before the crowds arrive or after 1 pm.

When choosing your hors d'œuvres, bear in mind that unless it is something you can eat with reasonable speed – your main course may get cold. There are microwave ovens at hand if this happens.

Tap water is free - you will find carafes and glasses on the bar near the coffee machine.

Chapter 15

Hotels

Bergerac has not enough hotels to cope with the increasing number of tourists arriving each year.

There are three hotels right in the centre of Bergerac – almost next door to each other in Place Gambetta. One is for tourism but the other two cater very well for the commercial businessmen visiting Bergerac.

The big problem is parking. There is very little 'free space' and restrictions are made because there are two markets each week – using up this space.

The traffic in Bergerac is getting worse and worse and now with all the people flying into Bergerac from eight different destinations in the UK, hiring cars, you must take parking into consideration.

At the moment, a large underground car park is being constructed and should be opened shortly but just like the parking facilities at the airport – they haven't been made big enough to cope with the influx of tourists. So if you decide to stay in town, think carefully about parking.

I have stayed in all three hotels. The only one with a restaurant is the Hotel de France but there are some super little restaurants [see 'Restaurant' chapter] in the vieux quartier which is about a seven minute walk.

The Hotel de France is the oldest – still standing - and mentioned in the Berry Bros father's wine book of many years ago. This hotel has a restaurant and swimming pool but is fairly expensive for what it has to offer.

The other hotels – mainly chain - are a fair distance from the centre of town and I suppose the nearest is the Hotel Verotel on the airport road which is about one kilometre into town – okay for the fittest!

The other three are on the west side of Bergerac – near the shopping centre, La Cavaille. The Kyriad has a swimming pool but the Campanile and the Etap are more for overnight stays. All three are handy for shopping and there is a bus service into town from outside the supermarket.

On the north side, on the Route to Perigueux, there are a couple of very good hotels with excellent cuisine but these are more for people looking for luxury accommodation and not so interested in going to town.

Hotel Flambée

49 ave Marceau Feyry

24100 Bergerac

Email   laflambee@laflambee.com

Tel: 05 53 57 52 33

Fax: 05 53 61 07 57

This is one of the top hotels in Bergerac. Unfortunately, it is well out of town on the road to Perigueux. The setting is most attractive – in the heart of Pecharmant vineyards – ideal for spending a few leisurely days sitting at the poolside.

The restaurant is extremely highly rated with an excellent five course lunch menu for around 35 euros - and the wine list includes many of the quality wines of Bergerac.

Le Manoir du Grand Vignoble

24140 Saint Julien de Crempse

Tel.   05 53 24 23 18

Fax :   05 53 24 20 89

Email: info@manoirdugrandvignoble.com

The hotel is a member of the Chateaux and hotels de France and is perfect if you are interested in horse riding. It is not very easy to find as it is off the beaten track but if you take the road to Perigueux and on just leaving Bergerac you will see a sign on your left to Saint Julien de Crempse. Follow this sign and you will eventually see the hotel.

Chateau des Vigiers Golf and Country Club

24240 Monestier
France
Tel: 05 53 61 50 00
Fax: 05 53 61 50 20
Email: reception@vigiers.fr

Going south west of Bergerac you will find what I suppose is the most luxurious hotel and that is the Chateau des Vigiers which is a golf club with lots of facilities, swimming pool, fitness centre, chalets and properties for those keen golf enthusiasts.

Unfortunately, as someone who specialises in food and wine and having been fortunate to have dined in some of the best restaurants in France, I find the cuisine offered in both restaurants lacks the finesse one would expect in such a well-appointed setting and the wine list also needs careful study.

Hotel Verotel

18 rue de Agen
24100 Bergerac
Tel: 05 53 24 89 76
Web: www.hotelverotel.fr

This is a modern hotel a few minutes from the airport on the left of the road into town. Reasonably priced and quiet. There is no problem with parking or having a quiet night's sleep – unlike the centre of town when the noise can start from about 6am.

Walking into town can take you 15 minutes but there is a cosy family run restaurant at the hotel.

Hotel Campanile

La Cavaille sud
Tel: 05 53 57 86 10
Fax: 05 53 57 72 21

These motels were very popular at one time and extremely reasonable for an overnight stay but in recent years the prices have crept up and although some may not agree with me, I think they are becoming quite expensive.

What I like best about the motel is that there is a bath which after travelling is ideal for the old soak.........

The Hotel Campanile in Bergerac is opposite the supermarket La Caveille on the west side of the town. It is about a 30-minute walk into town. There is a restaurant in the motel but also one on the opposite side of the road and of course, the Cafeteria in the supermarket.

Hotel Etap

Rte de Bordeaux
La Cavaille
24100 Bergerac
Tel: 05 53 22 80 00

This is the latest addition to the hotel list in Bergerac and is proving to be very popular as an overnight or weekend stop. The simple breakfast which is offered is good value

It is an economy hotel but is on the right side of the busy Bordeaux/Bergerac main road next to the Shopping Centre.

This hotel is bed and breakfast only, but there is the Campanile restaurant opposite and the 'Buffalo Grill' next door. You also have the Cafeteria in the supermarket which is open until ten at night serving freshly cooked food.

Hotel Kyriad

Route de Bordeaux
24100 Bergerac
Tel: 05 53 57 22 23
Fax: 05 53 58 25 24

This hotel was the first to be built after the new supermarket was built. To get to it you have to go on about another half kilometre past the supermarket roundabout.

The hotel was originally the Hotel Climat, a favourite moderately priced hotel chain. There is a swimming pool and restaurant. I have heard from neighbours that the dinner is quite good value.

Centre Ville

Hotel de Bordeaux [with swimming pool]
38 place Gambetta
Tel: 05 53 57 12 83
Fax: 05 53 57 72 14

Hotel de France [with swimming pool]

18 Pl Gambetta
24100 Bergerac
Tel :   05 53 57 11 61
Fax :   05 53 61 25 70
Web: www.hoteldefrance-bergerac.com

Hotel de Commerce

36 Pl Gambetta
24100 Bergerac
Tel :   0553273050
Fax :   0553582382
Web: www.hotl-du-commerce24.fr

Winewoman @Bergerac.France

Helen Gillespie-Peck

Title:
**Winewoman@
Bergerac.France**

Author:
Helen Gillespie-Peck

Publisher:
Melrose Books

ISBN:
978-0-954848-09-5

Format:
**Deluxe Hardback
With Full Colour
Dust Jacket.**

Size:
234 x 156mm

Price:
£16.99

MELROSE
BOOKS
Est. 1969

Helen Gillespie-Peck is a British wine writer and educator who has lived in Bergerac, France for more than thirty years. *Winewoman@Bergerac.France* is a culmination of her many years of experience in the world of wine and life in rural France.

Winewoman begins with the purchase of a 'new ruin' farmhouse in Bergerac. Chasing the French rural idyll, the author soon discovers that her dilapidated home would benefit more from a rebuild than a simple restoration. Electrical blackouts and invasions of livestock are regular features whilst a shower constructed from a large wine container was the sole concession to luxury. However, despite this, her passion for wine develops.

Winewoman is at once a readable, evocative biography and a comprehensive guide to wine producing areas and their vintages. *Winewoman* provides a wealth of interesting material including handy tips for wine storage and a glossary of the baffling terms printed on bottle labels. After reading *Winewoman* even the novice will know the difference between *Methode Rurale* and *Methode Traditionelle*.